Survey of Research in Economics on North East India (1970-1990)

Nirankar Srivastav

2026
Regency Publications
A Division of
Astral International Pvt. Ltd.
New Delhi – 110 002

First Published, 2000

Reprinted, 2026

ISBN: 978-81-87498-13-1 (Hardback)

Published by : **Regency Publications**
A Division of
Astral International Pvt. Ltd.
– ISO 9001:2015 Certified Company –
4736/23, Ansari Road, Darya Ganj
New Delhi-110 002
Ph. 011-43549197
E-mail: info@astralint.com
Website: www.astralint.com

Printed at : **Replika Press Pvt. Ltd.**

Research is to see
What every body else has seen,
But to think
What no one else has thought

FOREWORD

With the publication of this *Survey of Research in Economics on North East India (1970–1990)* by Dr. Nirankar Srivastav, we complete the review of published literature in the academic disciplines of Geography, Political Science, Sociology, History and Economics that the Advisory Committee of the NERC-ICSSR at its meeting held on November 22, 1991 had decided to sponsor. Earlier we have brought out four monographs in this series entitled—i) *Survey of Research in Political Science on North East India (1970–1990)* by Professor L.S. Gassah; ii) *Survey of Research in Sociology and Social Anthropology in North East India (1970–1990)* by Nikhlesh Kumar; iii) *Survey of Research in Geography on North East India (1970–1990)* by Dr. A.K. Bhagabati and Bimal K. Kar; and, iv) *Survey of Research in History on North East India (1970–1990)* by Dr. David R. Syiemlieh. The publication of the present monograph, however, does not exhausts all Social Science disciplines. Advisory Committee of the NERC, I hope, will consider sponsoring Surveys in the remaining areas of Social Sciences soon.

The Survey of Research in Economics on North East India was entrusted to Dr. Nirankar Srivastav of the Department of Economics, North Eastern Hill University, Shillong, sometime back. We are thankful to him not only for accepting our offer to undertake this work but also for completing it well before the deadline fixed. Dr. Srivastav has a number of publications to his credit. He Surveys the Researches in Economics in ten different sections. These thematic sections, thereafter, review publications chronologically. His classification may not be acceptable to all the possibly he has his own reasons. It appears from this study that certain areas of Economics have not been able to attract the attention of scholars and students of North East India as compared to others. It may be taken note off by both teachers and researchers alike. I hope that the work will be found useful by all those interested in the Researches in Economics in North East India. I also hope that the work will be received well like the previous surveys in the series.

Shillong
Dated: 21 February 2000

Jai Prakash Singh
Hon. Director
NERC - ICSSR

PREFACE

The book *Survey of Research in Economics on North East India* (1970–1990) is the outcome of the project assigned to me by the Indian Council of Social Science Research, North-Eastern Regional Centre, Shillong. The basic objective of this exercise is to review the literature in Economics, in the form of research dissertations, books and articles published in the journals during the period of twenty years (1970–1990).

The vast amount of literature produced during these two decades is scattered in the libraries of the various institutions in region. Under the constraints of the logistics, I could only cover the libraries in Shillong, Guwahati and Itanagar. The efforts were also, made to write the letters to the librarians, eminent economists and research scholars of the region to render relevant information and reprints of their valuable contributions to be included in this survey work. Response to this was not very encouraging, but some scholars and economists did respond and took the pains to send the photocopies of their research publications, abstracts, list of references and cross-references. This survey is enriched by their valuable contributions.

The present exercise is a humble one and by no means complete. Inevitably, the survey of this type has to dependent on the material that is available and accessible. All possible efforts are made, but there might be some important work, which are not known to the author and hence couldn't be covered in this survey. In this category the information related to M.Phil. dissertations, their titles, authors and years of award was not available so could not be included in this survey.

The work presents a systematic and chronological order of research work on various aspects of economics in north-east India and put it in proper perspective along with an inter-connected account of major issues that got attention of the various social scientists time to time. The analysis is also helpful in finding out the research gaps to be fulfilled in near future. Over and above, this work presents a bird's eye view of the development of economics as a discipline in the region. I hope that those who are interested in carrying out research on this subject and region will find this work useful.

I would like to offer my sincere thanks to the Chairman, the Honorary Director and Deputy Director of ICSSR (NERC), Shillong for giving me an opportunity to produce this work.

Shillong
March 2000

Nirankar Srivastav
Department of Economics
North-Eastern Hill University
Shillong 793 014

CONTENTS

INTRODUCTION

A survey of research in Economics, sponsored by the Indian Council of Social Science Research (ICSSR), New Delhi, is published in 1980. This survey work is available in seven volumes under following broad titles: Methods and Techniques; Macro Economics; Agriculture (in two volumes); Industry; Infrastructure and Econometrics. This work broadly covers the period up to 1970 and includes most of the research work in the fields of economics at national level.

As this work covers the entire nation, so studies on North East India couldn't get proper space. Moreover, it has reviewed the literature in Economics up till 1970 only. So, there is a need to have a separate review, which covers the period later than 1970 and confines itself to the north-eastern region of India. In this perspective, the North Eastern Regional Centre (NERC) of ICSSR, Shillong initiated a discipline-specific series of review of research literature on North-East India, generated during 1970–1990. The research literature to be reviewed is specified as, in the form of research dissertations, books and articles published in the journals.

This work presents a systematic and chronological survey of research work on various aspects of Economics in North East India. The basic purpose of this survey is to put the research work in proper perspective and an inter-connected account of major issues that got attention of the various social scientists from time to time.

The north-eastern region of India comprises seven states, namely, Assam, Meghalaya, Manipur, Nagaland, Tripura, Mizoram and Arunachal Pradesh. This part of India constitutes a strategic region, both by virtue of its location, surrounded by wide international borders and also because of predominant tribal population. Out of these seven states, four states, namely, Meghalaya, Arunachal Pradesh, Nagaland and Mizoram are the hill states, while the remaining three states—Assam, Tripura and Manipur are having both plain and the hill areas. Societies in the region are differentiated on the basis of those living in plain and those living on hills. Their respective economies are also significantly different.

The north-eastern region constitutes an area of 7.8 per cent and had 3.88 per cent of total population of India. It represents an average population density of 104 persons per square kilometre. Assam due to its location had the largest population in the region with an average density of 254 persons per square kilometre. It was followed by the states of Tripura, Manipur, Meghalaya, both in total number and density of population. The rate of growth of population in the region has remained continuously higher than national average. It is mainly due to the high birth rate, low death rate and heavy influx of immigrants in this region. Almost, 98.74 per cent of total area and 84 per cent of the total population of north east is rural in character as per 1981 Census.

The population of this region is heterogeneous composed of diverse races, religions, castes, languages and cultures which resulted in the growth of various types of social institutions and different economic activities of the people. The economy of the region is basically and predominantly agricultural having both food and cash crops. Agricultural production has not been able to keep pace with the growth of population and corresponding increase in demand. As a result the region has to import food grains from other states.

North East India is very rich in natural resources. It contains a variety of resources belonging to the basic natural components of land, water, forest, mineral and wild life. During the British rule attempts were initiated to explore and exploit some of these resources. Consequently, the tea, coal and natural oil industries were developed. But in spite of a fairly long history of industrial growth and availability of required potential raw materials, the region continues to be one of least developed regions of the country in terms of industrialisation. Different parts of region are at different stages of socio-economic development, some pastoral, some in primitive agricultural, some emerging with small-scale industries with rich handicrafts, and certain areas come with high and sophisticated technology in modern industrial sector.

The specificities of the north east region due to peculiar location and historical and socio-political background has affected a lot the development of institutions and economy. For this reason the nature of the economy of north east is significantly different in many ways than the regional economies of rest of India. This has attracted the attention of a large number of social scientists to study the various aspects of north eastern region economies time to time. Attempts have been made to identify the region specific economic problems and sort out the issues involved in defining the problems. In the process of reviewing the research literature, it was noticed that a serious and purposeful research of various economic issues of the north east available only after India's independence and more particularly since the beginning of economic planning in the country.

The concerted efforts in the direction of research in Economics got momentum after the establishment of Gauhati University in 1948, which is the first University of the region. Later on Dibrugarh University established in 1965, Assam Agricultural University in 1968, North-Eastern Hill University in 1972 and Manipur University in 1981. Some research works and economic survey is also conducted by the Agricultural and Economic Research Centre, Jorhat established in 1960.

Economics being a very important branch of social science, has been a very popular subject among the students and researchers, as almost all the universities have an independent post-graduate department of Economics, since very beginning of the university. It is worthwhile to mention that Economics contributed towards the largest number of research work among the total number of researches in social sciences.

Some efforts are made earlier to explore the status of socio-economic research in north eastern region at micro-level, for example, Alam (1990, 94). Srivastav (1998) made an attempt to highlight some trends of research in Economics in north eastern India. But there is a need to pursue a more systematic and detailed survey of regional research work in the fields of economics to understand the direction and dimensions of economic studies on north east. Nevertheless, this type of comprehensive survey is not the easy task, as the concerned studies are highly scattered and very limited in circulation.

In this connection, the efforts of NERC of ICSSR, Shillong are praiseworthy to take lead and decided to bring out the review of studies in Economics along with other disciplines of social sciences of north east India for the period of 1970–1990. The present survey would highlight the major economic issues which has drawn the attention of researchers and thus would be helpful to find out the research gaps to be fulfilled in near future. Over and above, this detail survey will present a bird's eye view of the development of economics as a discipline in north eastern region.

As mentioned earlier the research literature produced in these twenty years is scattered in the libraries of various universities/institutions of the region. It was not practically possible for the individual researcher to personally visit these libraries within the short period of time. The second best alternative was chosen to write the letters to the librarians, eminent economists and research scholars of the region to render their valuable contribution towards this survey work. Response to this effort was not very encouraging, but some scholars and economists did respond and took the pains to send the photocopies of their research publications, abstracts, list of references and cross references to the author. This survey is enriched by their valuable contributions. Of course, some of the important libraries of Shillong, Gauhati and Itanagar were personally visited by the author.

Another practical difficulty faced by the author was that some of the research works by nature were interdisciplinary and so intimately interwoven with other branches of social sciences like Sociology, Geography, Anthropology, History, and Commerce, that it was not very easy task to put them in proper perspective and classify them in a particular branch of Economics.

At the outset, it is to be confessed that this survey is neither complete, nor exhaustive and comprehensive, because efforts of an individual researcher, naturally, set the limit. Inevitably, the survey of this type has to be dependent on the material that is available and accessible. All possible efforts are made, but there might be some important work which are not known to the author and hence could not be covered in this survey. Verily, the ocean of knowledge has many more gems than one can retrieve and sky has many more stars that one can count or classify. However, the individual efforts are significant and relevant, as in this survey, as an additional source of available information and meant to be an informative source about the state of research in the fields of Economics in north east India. For the sake of convenience and from the utility point of view this report is arranged in twelve sections,. according to ten standard branches of Economics. Tenth section, also contains a brief review of research work available in the form of doctoral dissertations submitted to the various north eastern universities of the region in the field of Economics during the period 1970–1990.

References

Alam, K. (1990), "Status, Problems and Prospects of Socio-Economic Research in the North Eastern Region", *Journal of North-East India Council for Social Science Research*, 14:2, October, 27–39.

Alam, K. (1994), "Twenty Years of Research in Economics in the North East", *Journal of North-East India Council for Social Science Research*, Bi-Decennial Celebration of NEICSSR Issue, June, 16–25.

Indian Council for Social Science and Research (1980), *A Survey of Research in Economics* (Seven Volumes), Allied Publishers Pvt. Ltd., New Delhi.

Srivastav, N. (1998), "Some Trends of Research in Economics in North Eastern India", Singh, J.P., et al. (eds.), *Trends in Social Science and Humanities in North East India*, (1947–97), Regency Publications, New Delhi, 47–67.

I

AGRICULTURAL ECONOMICS

The economy of north eastern region of India is primarily agriculture based economy. More than 60 per cent of working population is earning their livelihood from agricultural sector. The prevailing agricultural practices, range from primitive (shifting cultivation) in hill areas to settled cultivation in plain areas. The pace of modernisation of agricultural sector is rather slow and peasant farming still exists in the region. As this sector is dominating the region's economy, it is obvious that issues related to agriculture have drawn a considerable amount of attention of the economists of the region. Their main research contributions are arranged in chronological order to view the agricultural scenario of the region.

The agricultural sector is not only satisfying the basic needs of food, but is also a provider of livelihood of large size of population. Goswami and Saikia (1970) identify the issues related to problems of agricultural development in tribal areas. A strong association is established between total crop output and marketed surplus. But the tribal inhabitant areas face altogether different type of problems of adaptability and responsiveness towards development activities undertaken by the various agencies.

A large number of policy measures are suggested by agricultural scientists and economists to improve the agricultural productivity, factor productivity so that agricultural sector could be transformed from stage of subsistence level to a profit making economic sector. One such approach is to adopt intensive area development program at village level.

In this context, Gohain (1970) investigated the institutional factors which work as deterrent for economic development in tribal areas. It was noticed that the socio-economic organisations and systems which are prevailing for a long period in a society, affect the behavioural pattern of people to a large extent. This behaviour is reflected in the forms of habit, tradition, work culture, customs and other human interactions. It was found that such factors are more intense and strong in a close society in tribal dominated areas.

In a subsistence economy, the agricultural sector hardly produces any surplus, similarly, agricultural income is also determined by low productivity and almost perfectly elastic supply of labour. Phukan and Burgohain (1972) determined the extent of surplus income in rural areas of Assam. Author also categorised the major agricultural practices prevailing in the region, on the basis of technology. Borah (1979) asserts in evolving the crop patterns under these two types of cultivations in Garo Hills district of Meghalaya.

Khaund (1970) discusses the various aspects related to agricultural sector in developing economies. For example, what is the role of agriculture? What should be the strategy for the development of agricultural sector? How the income distribution pattern changes and what is their significance in a society which is in the process of transition? In another important study, Khaund (1974) deals with the problem of rural unemployment. The different types of unemployment are prevailing in the rural areas of the region. An attempt has been made to measure the under employment in agricultural sector.

The North Eastern Region of India, is characterised primarily by two types of agricultural practices—settled agriculture in the plain and valley section; and the shifting (Jhum) cultivation in hilly sections of the region. Jhum cultivation is a primitive form of agricultural practice, involving the clearing of forests, bushes etc., to slump level. It is allowed to dry up and the residue is burnt up. The fields are prepared by clearing and await the on set of the rains. After which seeds are sown and crops cultivated. These fields are temporary as they are used only for one or two seasons; after that the same process is repeated in adjacent forest areas. In other words, there is a distinct rotation of fields that averages 3 to 10 years. This period is known as Jhum cycle.

The Jhum practice had formed an important element of the involved person's perceptions, traditions and socio-economic relations. These features have attracted a large number of social scientists to study the various aspects of Jhum cultivation. In this sequence, Saha (1970) made an attempt to explain the concept of carrying capacity of shifting cultivation. This study analyses data from three villages in North Eastern India—one each from Karbi hills, Garo hills and Mizo hills. Estimations of farm productivity suggest that depending upon the quality of land, only three to nine persons per square km, can be maintained through Jhuming at a subsistence level, at the existing level of productivity, provided fifty per cent of the total area is available for cultivation and 15 to 20 years are provided for the Jhum cycle. Empirical evidences show that the population density in the hill areas under study has exceeded the carrying capacity under the prevailing system of the cultivation. This is indicative of the extreme poverty of hill people and their low level of living.

The cultivators, who practice Jhum cultivation are known as 'Jhumias'. Mishra (1976) discusses the socio-economic status of the Jhumias in Tripura state. Author observes, the existence of various classes within the Jhumias as per their prevailing socio-economic status. Accordingly, more enterprising Jhumias; belonging to Sardar class were properly linked with the cash economy through the sale of forest products. The lower class of Jhumias are still associated with barter economy. This way author studies the scope and extent of socio-economic adjustments, the dynamics of social relationships among the Jhumias.

Attempts to classify the north-east on the basis of agricultural practices and performance and formulate planning strategies for agricultural development in the region are still in their infant stage. However, Barman and Das (1978) analysed the regional variation in the distribution of farm population with a view of highlighting the problem of population pressure on the limited land resources. Using suitable quantitative methods authors identifiy the agricultural regions in Assam. It is a worth noting attempt to regionalise the state of Assam on the basis of crop-association pattern.

A reasonably good inter disciplinary work in the form of collection of articles, on shifting cultivation is available in a volume edited by Datta-Ray (1980). This volume is based on the research articles presented to a seminar organised by North East India Council for Social Science Research (NEICSSR), Shillong, on shifting cultivation in North-East India. Most of the social scientists contributed paper to the volume, are of the opinion that shifting cultivation is a way of life of the Jhumias. Bose (1980) and Bhowmic (1980) both expressed that shifting cultivation is the natural way of life of the involved tribal people in a form that it is a major source of earning of their lively hood. Ganguli (1980) explained in detail the issues which relate the Jhuming with the various aspects of life like values, attitudes and beliefs of Jhumias. It was noted that the entire life of the Jhumias, i.e., society, polity and culture, revolves around this form of agriculture. Aspects of agricultural growth and land distribution pattern are studied by Guhathakurta (1981) for the state of Meghalaya. Factors such as agricultural productivity, yield per hectare and their temporal variations are discussed in this study. Agricultural growth has also been associated with land distribution patterns, in order to study the prospects of economic development of the state.

Ganguli (1982) describes a 'conceptual model of Jhuming' as a frame of reference for studying the effect of Jhum failure of 1981 in Tripura, on the Jhum system of the state. Author identifies three main characteristics of Jhumias: (i) Jhum cultivation doesn't depend on the use of productive inputs or consumption of side produced goods or disposal of produced goods outside the Jhum economy; (ii) production is for subsistence only; (iii) Jhuming takes place in a uni-class frame work of a society. It concludes that, in the event of Jhum failure, the Jhum economy can not remain self sufficient. Jhumias have to either depend on forest economy or outside borrowings or state relief measures for their survival. This paper generated an interesting debate among regional economists and other social scientists. Samanta (1982) attempts to assess the perception of tribal farmers in Tripura about the shifting or settled cultivation. This study is based on an extensive field survey of the tribal households of two villages belonging to Tripuri tribe of two development blocks of West Tripura district. It was found that the villages, who practice both shifting and settled cultivation, only 26 per cent of villagers expressed the opinion that they should practice Jhum cultivation along with settled cultivation, because their forefathers practised it. Round about 20 per cent of villagers only, opined that leaving Jhum cultivation means breaking their traditions. Study proposes that majority of Jhum cultivators are ready to adopt the settled cultivation, provided long term incentives are offered to cover the risk and uncertainties.

Dasgupta (1983) presents a modified version of 'conceptual model of Jhuming' developed earlier by Ganguli (1982). In a more realistic approach, author propounds that in the event of a Jhum failure it is going to spell disaster only for the Jhumias, who are at the subsistence level, while the Jhumias, who are better off may even gain from it. So, Jhum economy in the present context has lost its closed character. This mathematical model needs empirical testing to get support from ground reality. Ganguli (1983), while taking part in the debate replied to the most of the questions raised by Dasgupta (1983), and in support of his 'closed economy' assumptions, he suggests that if there are so-called Jhumias, who are well-to-do and produce surplus, accumulate and involved in money lending business, then they don't belong to the Jhum system of her model. In fact, such Jhumias exist outside the closed and subsistence Jhum system.

Adhikari (1983) expressed a few valid comments on the paper, of Dasgupta (1982) and point out that Dasgupta (1982) ignores two basic factors in her model (a) when Jhum crop fails income from other operations can also be increased; (b) the role of state sponsored developmental schemes, Tribal Area Autonomous District councils and other financial credit institutions. In this light it is suggested that the problem of Jhum failure needs to be analysed in a broad frame work of general crop failure. In author's opinion, the impact of natural calamities upon the Jhumias differ from that upon settled cultivators only in regard to magnitudes.

Peasant agriculture, the dominant feature of the agrarian economy of Assam, the geographical terrain, the existing land tenure system and the tradition orientation of the peasant have been the major contributing factors for this primitive type of agriculture. Das (1984) traced the history of land reform in Assam and highlighted the problems caused by small and fragmented land holdings in the performance of agriculture. Author discusses the structural basis of the peasantry. The basic objective of this study is to analyse the socio-economic structure of peasantry and spatial pattern of peasant agriculture in the state. Study also, investigates the institutional factors like the existing laws of inheritance, the strong hold of religion along with family size, class and caste structure of peasantry. Turning to the agro-economic aspects, the author examines the land tenure system and land-labour-capital relationships. The study reveals that there is lack of almost all the infrastructural facilities like electrification, irrigation, agricultural credit, transport communication and marketing facility in rural Assam. Agricultural economists and other social scientists would find this work very valuable.

The rate of growth and pattern of agricultural development indicate the economic dynamism of an agrarian area. While the meaning of agricultural growth is straight and easy to understand, agricultural development is multidimensional in nature and renders difficulty in conceptualisation, as well as application of appropriate methods for analysis. While assessing various facts of agricultural development Bhagwati (1984) developed a conceptual model in order to identify the complex pattern of agricultural development in Assam. Author treated crop productivity to be a vital aspect of agricultural development, and therefore, included as an important component of model.

Bhagwati (1985) undertakes a well-organised work on land use and land classification in the Brahmaputra valley of Assam. Author tries to present the picture of land use in the region. Based on secondary data, this work provides some useful clues towards land use problems of the region.

Saikia and Phukan (1985) present a book, containing the main findings of the research projects completed by the Agro-Economic Research Centre for North-East India, Assam Agricultural University, since its inception in 1960 to December 1985. The book is divided into three sections: (i) Reports on point village survey, (ii) Reports on village survey, (iii) summaries of problem oriented studies. The statistical profile of North-East India is, presented at the end of the book related to area and population, area production and yield of crops for the states of North East India for the year 1982–83.

A study based on extensive field survey of tribal dominated villages of Tripura, mainly practice Jhum cultivation, is available with Dasgupta and Banerjee (1984). Field work for the study conducted by incorporating more than two thousand households, which is in fact, a fairly large sample size. This study is important in a sense, that its findings are contradictory with the findings of the studies earlier done by the scholars in the same field. Earlier studies univocally propound that Jhum cultivation is a way of life for Jhumias, while the present study found that most of the Jhumias are ready to give up Jhum cultivation if better alternative/options are given to them in a form of continuous government assistance. This concludes that economic, social and cultural nature of Jhum were of less importance in the world view of Jhumias for continuing this practice. Study cited strong empirical evidences in favour of its arguments and conclusions.

Saikia (1988) evaluated the agricultural development in Assam during the plan period. This study is primarily based on the time series data for the period 1950–51 to 1975–77, on production and productivity of the major crops in Assam. It was noticed that growth rate of agricultural output was, by and large, due to increase in area. Rural electrification is considered as one of the important factors to accelerate the development of agricultural sector. On the other hand, farmers were also, not interested to have electricity driven irrigation pumps. Author also, highlight reasons of slow agricultural growth such as, existence of small holdings and other socio-economic constraints.

Agarwal (1988) studied the problems of shifting cultivators and observes that the Jhumias getting assistance in work from other fellow-villagers are finding it difficult on exchange basis due to change in the attitude of people and introduction of the use of paid labour. One of the crucial factors of failures in Jhum control is the lack of commercialisation due to lack of marketing and transportation facilities in the rural areas. The customary property rights and land ownership are also analysed in this context.

Saikia (1989) examined the role of women in agriculture in Assam and found that except when driven by acute economic hardship females in this region by and large, don't go for wage employment. They mostly work in their own farms. The average employment of female labour for marginal, small and medium farmers in days per hectare of gross cropped area is found to be very low. Similarly, the extent of utilisation of female labour as proportion to total working days available in farm work in one year is also very low. This suggests that the contribution of female workers in agricultural production depends on sex division of work. It is high time to recognise the importance of female labour and its rational utilisation by developing skill and imparting education.

Upadhyaya (1989) probes size-productivity relation and capitalist development in the agricultural economy of two villages of Mizoram, through a sample study of one hundred families for the year 1986–87. It concludes that, when small holding farms appear very productive, it is because the farmers put their own labour in it. Author incorporates this fact and adjusted the estimation of farm productivity accordingly. The study also noticed traces of capitalist farming within the sample villages.

Most of the studies, however, dealing particularly with the developmental aspects of agriculture are discussing number of factors, which affect the agriculture in North-East Region. But very few studies are based on ecological aspect of agriculture. One such attempt is made by Goswami (1989), in ecology-oriented study, discusses the various aspects of floods and its impact on agriculture of Assam. Author suggests and recommends the reorganisation of the cropping pattern and crop rotation according to the flood environment to ensure sustainable development of agriculture.

Barah (1990) analyses the geo-political and agro-climatological factors in order to explain the economic backwardness of the economy of Assam. Author has explained with the help of statistics like compound rate of growth, distribution of operational holdings, comparative growth rates of area production and yield, pattern of regional and average seasonal rainfall, composition of soil, per hectare profitability, cost of production and damage due to flood, that the performance of agricultural sector is poor. Furthermore, industrial sector is underdeveloped and growth of service sector is very slow and haphazard. It is concluded that the region has vast potential for agricultural development due to availability of rich natural endowments. Unless access to the rest of India be improved further, the modernisation of agricultural sector on wider scale would be difficult to attain.

Mishra and Howbora (1990) made an attempt to account for differences in agricultural productivity due to institutional factors. In a case study, authors observe that institutional factors play an important role in determining agricultural productivity and land utilisation in the study area. This research paper is based on extensive field survey and collected primary data from the interior villages of North Lakhimpur Development Block of Assam.

Phukan (1990) presents a book on agricultural developments in Assam. The purpose of this study is to understand the nature of agriculture and analyse the process of agricultural development in Assam from 1950–51 to 1984–85, a period of thirty-five years of planned development efforts. He examines the various issues like distribution of land, labour and capital and their relationship to crop output. Further, it takes note of transitional phases of agricultural systems and the role of developmental efforts. Empirical evidences are used in identifying the main factors responsible for slow rates of growth of output, productivity and farm efficiency. This book is useful to students, research scholars and teachers associated with agricultural economics and economic development and planning.

References

Adhikari, O.S. (1983), "Anatomy of a Jhum Failure: A Few Comments", *The Journal of the North East India Council for Social Science Research*, Vol. 8, No. 2, October, 10–12.

Agarwal, A.K. (1988), From Jhum to Settled Cultivation, Commerce (Weekly), Vol. 157, 18–19.

Barah, B.C. (1990), "Constraints and Prospects of Economic Development of Assam: An Emphasis on Agricultural Sector", *Journal of the North East India Council for Social Science Research*, Vol. 14, No. 1, April, 1–21.

Barman, R. and Das, M.M. (1978), "Crop Combination Regions of Assam", *North Eastern Geographer*, Vol. 10, 15–22.

Bhagwati, A.K. (1984), "Levels of Agricultural Productivity in the Brahmaputra Valley: A Regional Analysis", *North Eastern Geographer*, Vol. 16, No. 1 and 2, 30–38.

Bhagwati, A.K. (1985), "Patterns of Land Utilisation in the Brahmaputra Valley", *Indian Journal of Landscape Systems and Ecological Studies,* Vol. 18, No. 2, 62–69.

Bhowmic (1980), "Shifting Cultivation: A Plea for New Strategy", in Dutta-Ray, B. (1980), 6–33.

Borah, D. (1979), "Patterns of Crop Production Under Shifting and Terrace Cultivation: A Case Study in Garo Hills", *Indian Journal of Agricultural Economics,* Vol. XXXIII, No. 4, 18–23.

Bose, S.C. (1980), "Development and Change in an Area Used Shifting Cultivation", in Dutta-Ray, B. (1980), 122–132.

Das, M.M. (1984), *Peasant Agriculture in Assam,* Inter-India Publications, New Delhi.

Dasgupta, Malabika (1983), "Anatomy of a Jhum Failure: Some Extensions", *The Journal of the North East India Council for Social Science Research,* Vol. 7, No. 1, April , 19–25.

Dasgupta, Malabika and Banerjee, A. (1984), "Jhumming as the Way of Life of the Jhumias: An Analysis of Data from Tripura", *Journal of the North East India Council for Social Science Research,* Vol. 8, No. 1, April 17–25.

Datta-Ray, B. (1980) (ed.), *Shifting Cultivation of North-East India,* North East Indian Council for Social Science Research (NEICSSR), Shillong.

Ganguli, J.B. (1983), "Operation of the Jhum Model", *The Journal of the North East India Council for Social Science Research,* Vol. 8, No. 2, October, 13–15.

Ganguli, J.B. (1980), "Socio-Economic Problems of Transition from Shifting to Secondary Cultivation", in Dutta-Ray, B. (1980), 28–39.

Ganguli, J.B. (1982), "Vulnerability of Jhumming as Closed System to National Calamities", *The Journal of the North East India Council for Social Science Research,* Vol. 9, No. 13, October, 9–13.

Gohain, D. (1970), "Institutional Factors as Deterrent for Economic Development in Tribal Areas", *Indian Journal of Agricultural Economics,* Vol. XXV, No. 3, 58–67.

Goswami, D.C. (1989), "Floods and Their Impact on the Agriculture of Assam", in Goswami, P.C. (ed.) *Agriculture of Assam,* Institute of Development Studies, Guwahati, Assam, 191–207.

Goswami, P.C. and Saikia, P.D. (1970), "Problems of Agricultural Development in Tribal Areas", *Indian Journal of Agricultural Economics,* Vol. XXV, No. 3, 23–31.

Guhathakurta, S.N. (1981), "Agricultural Growth and Land Distribution in Meghalaya", in Mathew, T. (ed.), *Tribal Economy of the North Eastern Region,* Spectrum Publications, Guwahati, 7–10.

Khaund, H.P. (1970), "Changes in Income Distribution Pattern and Their Significance in a Society in Transition", *Indian Journal of Agricultural Economics,* Vol. XVI, No. 3, 33–47.

Khaund, H.P. (1974), "Towards Measuring Under Employment in Agriculture", *Indian Journal of Agricultural Economics,* Vol. XIX, No. 3, 31–38.

Mishra, B.P. (1976), *Socio-Economic Adjustments of Tribals: A Case Study of Tripura Jhumias,* People's Publishing house, New Delhi.

Mishra, S.K. and Howbora, B. (1990), "Socio-Cultural Determinants of Agricultural Performance: A Case Study of Lakhimpur Block, Assam", in Rai, R.K. et al (eds.), Rawat Publishers, Jaipur, 125–134.

Phukan, U. and Borgohain, D.K. (1972), "The Study on Surplus Income in Rural Areas: A Study in Assam", *Indian Journal of Agricultural Economics*, Vol. XVIII, No. 1, 8–23.

Phukan, U. (1990), *Agricultural Development in Assam: 1950–1985*, Mittal Publications, New Delhi.

Saha, N. (1970), "Carrying Capacity of Shifting Cultivation", *Indian Journal of Agricultural Economics*, Vol. XXV, No. 3.

Saikia, A. (1989), "Role of Women in Agriculture: The Situation in Assam", in Saikia, P.D. and Phukan, U. (eds.) *Rural Development in North East India*, D.K. Publishing Distribution (P) Ltd., Delhi, 195–206.

Saikia, P.D. (1988), "Agricultural Development in Assam During Plan Periods", in Bhorali, D. (ed.), *Economic Development of North East Region*, Spectrum Publications, Guwahati, 82–90.

Saikia, P.D. and Phukan, U. (1985), "Twenty Years of Agro-Economic Research in NE India: 1960–85", Agro-Economic Research Centre for North East India, Jorhat, Assam.

Samanta, R.K. (1982), "Shifting or Settled Cultivation: Perception of Tribal Farmers in Tripura", *Man in India*, 62, 2, June, 180–190.

Sri Prakash and Tarujyoti (1990), "Sources of Agricultural Growth of North East India: A Case Study of Inter Crop and Inter Regional Variations", in Rai, R.K. et al. (eds.), *Hill Area Development: Issues and Perspectives*, Rawat Publications, Jaipur, 94–117.

Upadhyaya, K.K. (1989), "Size Productivity Relation and Captialist Development in Agriculture with Theoretical Underpinnings", *Indian Journal of Economics*, Vol. 69, No. 275, 389–404.

II

RURAL ECONOMICS

Rural Economics deals broadly with the understanding of the patterns and processes of various socio-economic phenomena and transformations which are taking place in rural areas of the region. In the context of the prevalence of highly diverse social phenomena such as caste, tribe, religion, language, literacy and education, rural economic studies on the north east assumes immense significance. It has received added importance because of the ongoing process of socio-economic interaction and transformation among different population groups of the region amidst the traditionally stronghold. In fact, a considerable number of studies on various rural economic issues, pattern and processes have been made in the north east since early eighties. The following section presents some of the studies in chronological order.

Agro-economic Research Centre, Jorhat, Assam, organised a seminar on the problems of research in tribal areas in February 1970. The present volume (Goswami, 1972) is the outcome of some selected papers contributed to this seminar. The papers are categorised in three heads such as—(a) social factors affecting economic development, (b) problems of field investigation in tribal areas, and (c) village study as a tool of socio-economic research in tribal areas. Most of the papers presented were empirical studies based on field survey and discuss the socio-economic life of different tribal communities of India. The students of Economics and other Social Sciences interested in studying tribal/rural economics based on intensive field survey may find this publication extremely useful.

Jafri and Sahu (1978) analysed the impact of Shillong city in its fringe areas in terms of social transformation and levels of social development. This is an attempt to study the levels of rural development as an impact of development in Shillong city. The analysis reveals that adjoining villages form a transitional zone between the completely rural hinterland and city proper.

Mathew (1980) edited a volume on economy of the North-East Region. The papers included in this volume were presented at a seminar on tribal economy held in March 1976. The seminar was organised by the Department of Economics, North-Eastern Hill University, Shillong. This volume contains altogether nineteen articles, covering wide coverage of issues related to status, problems and perspectives of economic development of the regional economies of NE India. Five papers are related to agricultural sector including Jhum cultivation. Two papers are on land reforms, four papers on Meghalaya's economy and one each on the economies of Nagaland, Mizoram and Arunachal Pradesh. In this book, authors have made a good attempt to investigate thoroughly the prevailing modes of production of the tribal economies of the region. The general feeling of the large number of contributors is that any attempt to transform the existing mode of production requires the understanding of the nature, functions and inter-relationship of the economic structure with the other structural levels of society.

Goswami (1980) tries to explain the Economics of Jhum cultivation considering the various factors responsible for shifting cultivation and suggests the practical steps to control it. Author concludes that integrated approach based on an appropriate coordination among agriculture, animal husbandry, forestry, soil conservation, public works, irrigation and small scale industries departments of state would be necessary to wean away tribal people from jhum cultivation. Besides this, there is a need to generate the confidence among jhumias that they can have a better life without the jhum cultivation.

Wadia (1980) analyses the state efforts and their role in controlling jhum cultivation. The role of North-Eastern Council in this connection is also highlighted. Author suggests that the reclamation of lower and middle level cultivators for settled cultivation, horticulture crops, afforestation, rehabilitation of tribal families are a few measures that would help in controlling jhum.

Ganguli (1984) edited a volume on rural marketing in North-East India. This edited volume is the outcome of the papers presented to a seminar on problems of rural market and marketing in North-East India, organised by North East India Council for Social Science Research in April 1982 in Shillong. The book contains four subsections. The first part is on the theme of the emerging rural market structure in North East India containing ten research articles. Second part is devoted to the theme, marketing problems facing by handicrafts and handloom product producers. This part consists of eight articles. The seven case studies are discussed in the third part about marketing situations at various regions in the rural areas. Market as the focal point for social change, is the theme of fourth and last part of the book. This book presents a good picture of rural market structure of the region.

Sharma (1984) analyses the problems and prospects of marketing in tribal areas. Author is of the view that planning of marketing in the tribal areas is largely a question of establishing a suitable organisation and making effective administration arrangements. The basic principles which should govern the operational plan are: (i) Regulation of market economy; (ii) Stabilising the price; (iii) Establishing single point for purchase of commodities offered by the tribal and sale of important consumer commodities and agricultural inputs.

Sharma and Thakur (1984) discussed the problem of marketing among the plain tribes of Assam in the form of a case study of two Bodo-Kachari villages in Goalpara district of Assam. Analysing the land holding patterns of the individual families of these two villages, it is concluded that in the process of transition from production for self consumption to middle-men oriented production for exchange, many producers are alienated from their land and becoming landless, in this process and leading to the emergence of agricultural labour market in tribal areas.

A study based on a survey conducted by Agro-Economic Research Centre for North East India, Jorhat, in the two villages of East Khasi Hill district of Meghalaya, in 1979, taking a sample of fifty farm households, Bora (1984) found that the potato growing farmers don't get remunerative price for their produces. This is due to monopoly combination of wholesale buyers of Shillong. It is suggested that State government may announce a minimum support price for potato and other important crops to protect the interests of the farmers.

Roy Burman (1984) studied the working of Poverty Alleviation Programs in the states of Manipur and Nagaland. Basic objective of this area study is to evaluate the performance of Integrated Rural Development Program, National Rural Employment Program, and Rural Landless Employment Guarantee Schemes in the light of patterns of land and asset ownership, flow of credit, organisational and infrastructural requirements. Author concludes that inadequate development of infrastructural facilities, public delivery system and social consumption facilities are major hindrance in the efficient implementation of program. The present study also show that some of the communities of Nagaland and Manipur have by tradition controls and access to resources but they are not well-off. Keeping this in mind, author has made a number of suggestions to implement rural development programs more efficiently and effectively.

Ahmed (1987) made an attempt to study the autonomy of rural poverty in Assam. This is a micro level study based on primary statistics collected from six villages of Dibrugarh subdivision. The purpose of the study is not only to estimate the number of poverty-stricken people but also, to establish the link between rural poverty with family size, size of operational holdings, tenancy agreements, and under employment, asset holdings, indebtedness, dwelling conditions, pattern of rural consumption expenditure and rural infrastructural facilities. Author establishes that poverty being a multidimensional phenomenon, an efficient assault on it has also to be multidimensional and well integrated. This study is useful for researchers, in the field of economics, and policy makers and planners.

Saikia and Phukan (1989) edited a volume on Rural Development on North East India. This volume is the outcome of the papers presented to a seminar on the Problems of Rural Development of the Region. Seminar was organised by the Agro-Economic Research Centre for North East India, Assam Agricultural University, Jorhat, in March 1986, as a part of the Silver Jubilee celebration of the Centre (1960–85). An attempt has been made by the contributors to understand the process and problems of rural development through a multidisciplinary approach. The present volume consists of twenty two research papers with a resume, as twenty third chapter. The last chapter helps us to take a bird's eye view, a stock of the progress of rural development program in NE India and find out the factors inhibiting the development process.

Goswami (1989) reviewed the changes in the concept of rural development since pre-independence period to that of present time. Author highlights the difficulties involved in removing the poverty as cost of living is continuously rising, as a result of price rising. However, poverty can be reduced by making available the gainful employment to the poor. Analysing the Seventh Five-Year Plan outlay distribution, it was observed that expenditure on the implementation of the rural development program is not uniform throughout the nation, in fact, it shows a declining trend proportionately in the state, Assam.

Roy Burman (1989) raised some basic issues relating to the strategy of poverty alleviation in the Seventh Plan. Author surveyed the development experience of the other developing countries and expressed doubts whether the future of rural population can be changed within the prevailing socio-economic framework, i.e., under liberal capitalism.

For the purpose of effective implementation of rural development programs, the role of administrative set-up is very important. In this context, Maithani (1989) suggested an alternative model of organisational set-up consisting: (a) Unitary District Development Administration; (b) District Development Councils; (c) District/Local Level Governments. It further suggests a single combination of one set-up of all the heads of the departments under administrative framework of the Deputy Commissioner. Heavy reliance on administrative officials can be mitigated by associating the rural development programs with Pachayati Raj institutions.

Dutta (1989) studied the socio-economic changes in two sample villages of the Jorhat district of Assam between 1950–80. It was found that the resource base of the villages have not developed during past thirty years. There were marginal changes in cropping pattern but no significant increase in productivity of crops. Comparing the changes between Hindu caste dominated village with a Scheduled Caste dominated village, it was found that a Scheduled Caste dominated village developed at a slower pace. But there were significant improvements in the standard of living in the Hindu Caste dominated village due to more opportunities of salaried jobs.

Srivastav and Thomas (1990) have made a critical evaluation of the performance of Integrated Rural Development Program (IRDP) in Meghalaya. This evaluation highlights the prospects and constraints of this rural development program in the socio-economic milieu of Meghalaya. Study based on primary survey of the purposively selected development blocks, the IRDP beneficiaries are classified on the basis of family size, income, occupation and their relationships are discussed in the light of quality of assets, amount of working capital and income generated. Efforts are made to estimate the number of beneficiaries crossed the poverty line during the period of scheme.

References

Ahmed, A. (1987), *The Autonomy of Rural Poverty in Assam,* Mittal Publications and Distributors, Delhi.

Bhadra, R.K. (1979), "Rural Class Structure in Post-Independence Assam", *Economic and Political Weekly,* 14, 4 January, 165–167.

Bora, D. (1984), "Cultivation of Potato and its Marketing: Problems in Meghalaya", In Ganguli, J.B. (ed.), Omsons Publications, Guwahati.

Dutta, P.C. (1989), "Rural Change in Assam 1951–1981: A case Study", in Saikia and Phukan (eds.), D.K. Publishing and Distribution (P) Ltd., Delhi, 237–248.

Ganguli, J.B. (1984) (ed.), *Marketing in North East India,* Omsons Publications, Guwahati.

Goswami, P.C. (1972) (ed.), *Socio-Economic Research in Tribal Areas,* Agro-Economic Research Centre, Jorhat, Assam.

Goswami, P.C. (1980), "Problems of Jhum Control", in Mathew, T. (ed.), Spectrum Publications, Guwahati, 48–61.

Goswami, P.C. (1989), "Problems of Rural Development in North East India: An Overview", in Saikia and Phukan (eds.), D.K. Publishing and Distribution (P) Ltd., Delhi, 15–34.

Jafri, S.S.A. and Sahu, R. (1978), "Urban Fringe of Shillong City: A case Study of Levels of Rural Development", *Indian Journal of Regional Sciences,* Vol. 10, No. 2, 96–101.

Maithani (1989), "Organisational Design for Rural Development in North East Region", in Saikia and Phukan (eds.), D.K. Publishing and Distribution (P) Ltd., Delhi, 49–66.

Mathew, T. (1980) (ed.), *Tribal Economy of the North East Region*, Spectrum Publications, Guwahati.

Roy Burman, B.K. (1984), *Towards Poverty Alleviation Programmes in Nagaland and Manipur*, Mittal Publications and Distributors, Delhi.

Roy Burman, B.K. (1989), "Rural Development in the Seventh Plan: A Restatement of the Issues", in Saikia and Phukan (eds.), D.K. Publishing and Distribution (P) Ltd., Delhi, 1–14.

Saikia, P.D. and Phukan, U. (1989) (eds.), *Rural development in North East India*, D.K. Publishing and Distribution (P) Ltd., Delhi.

Sarma, J. (1979), "Barriers of Rural Development in Assam", *Economic and Political Weekly*, 14, 4 January, 27–32.

Sharma and Thakur (1984), "Problems of Marketing Among the Plain Tribes of Assam", in Ganguli, J.B. (ed.), Omsons Publications, Guwahati.

Sharma, B.D. (1984), "Marketing in Tribal Areas", in Ganguli, J.B. (ed.), Omsons Publications, Guwahati, 3–18.

Srivastav, N. and Thomas, E.D. (1990), "Integrated Rural Development Program in Meghalaya: A Critical Evaluation", in Rai, R.K. et al. (eds.), *Hill Area Development: Issues and Perspectives*, Rawat Publications, Jaipur, 188–194.

Wadia, F.K. (1980), "Control of Shifting Cultivation in the North Eastern Region", in Mathew, T. (ed.), Spectrum Publications, Guwahati, pp. 62–79.

III

LAND ECONOMICS

Land is one of the important factors of production is known from the ages for its unique and peculiar characteristics. It has been a major source of livelihood for the human beings. The growing population pressure, rising in economic activities and scarcity of land demands the optimum use of land. In order to pursue this goal, the detailed land use planning is very much needed. This required appropriate land accounting, mapping, and it's secotral use. State and local governments should ensure the micro and macro area planning to cater the long term requirements balancing the availability of land resources. Land use studies assume great significance particularly in the case of North East India as the region is remarkably diverse, both spatially and culturally. The regional economists attempted studies on land use of the region at micro and macro level.

Sinha (1984) draws attention to the fact that the heterogeneous size of the various states in India creates a number of social, economic and administrative problems. In the context of North East India, Assam is a bigger state, whereas, other north eastern states are smaller in size. The functional problems of small north eastern states can be understood under the following terms: implications of smallness (i) on the development in terms of resource availability; (ii) in terms of inter state linkages; (iii) in regional perspectives and expectations from the centre; (iv) in social context, as unique and small isolated marginal people; (v) in terms of manpower planning, in the light of high rate of immigration. These issues can play a vital role, while discussing the development strategy for these states.

Bora (1986) presents a study on the land utilisation patterns in the state, Assam over a period of twenty eight years from 1951–52 to 1978–79. It gives a clear picture of land utilisation pattern for all the plains districts of Assam. From the indepth analysis, various factors responsible for the changing pattern of land utilisation have emerged. Besides, a detailed discussion on the cropping pattern, crop intensity, crop rotation, production, yield and productivity, fragementation of holdings of land and the natural, socio-economic and infrastructural factors, which have great impact on land utilisation in the state, have also been included. The book also provides a brief description of historical evolution of land tenure, policies on land systems and land reforms in the state.

A micro level analysis, based on primary data collected from ten villages selected from Sibsagar and Nowgaon, has been included in the book. The primary focus of this study is to identify the factors affecting land utilisation by farms. This study also investigates the relationship between the cropping pattern and the size of holding and the influence of the level of irrigation on production and cropping intensity. This work will be of great help for the researchers interested in land and agricultural economics.

Dutta (1986) edited a volume on land use pattern in North East India. The research articles included in this volume were presented in the seminar on land in North East India. The book contains seventeen papers related various issues, like, land use under shifting cultivation, cropping patterns, soil fertility, eco-system, land use for live-stock production, and permanent cultivation, etc.

Adhikari (1986) presents a macro-economic model to understand the problem of land alienation and its economic consequences in North East India. The aim of the study is to build up a simple theoretical frame work which provides the possible explanation for the genesis of alienation, to predict the consequences and to provide some practical suggestions for solving the problem. This study requires an empirical testing with the help of primary data collected from the field.

A volume titled 'Land Reforms and Peasant Movement' edited by Goswami (1986) consists of almost two dozen research articles. As suggested by the title of book, the major theme of the papers are on land, land relations and reforms in the plain and valleys of north eastern region. This volume is the outcome of research papers presented in a seminar, held in April, 1984 under the auspicious of the North East India Council for Social Science Research, Shillong. This volume provides the readers with authentic information along with scientific analysis of the various issues relating to land use, land tenure system, status of land reforms and its impact, strucutral changes and changing patterns of agrarian relations in the region. This book is useful for the students and researchers interested in knowing the analytical view of land and agricultural pattern in the context of north eastern economy.

Neog and Bordoloi (1986) studied the relationship between distribution pattern of land holdings and planned agricultural development in the region. They have applied Lorenz curve approach and calculated Gini coefficient to ascertain the land holdings inequalities. This study is based on the secondary statistic published by world agricultural census of 1970–71 and 1976–77. It was found that there exists a significant level of inequality among marginal farms and this type of inequality is increased in 1976–77 compared with 1970–71 in all the state of North East except in Tripura. The estimated Gini concentration ratios show an increase over time in concentration of land holdings in Arunachal Pradesh and Meghalya and decrease in Tripura. Authors argued that, other things being equal, reduction of inequality is expected to get better results in terms of higher productivity.

Agarwal (1986) traces the transition from traditional system of community ownership of land to the emerging new system of individual ownership in Arunachal Pradesh. It is observed that with the opening up of this frontier tribal dominated state and the consequent flow of cash into it, a small class of moneyed tribals have emerged, who in the absence of alternative avenues for investment, are most likely to ulilise their money in purchasing of land, leading to further concentration of land in fewer hands, if remedial measures are not taken in time.

Mali (1989) analysed in his book, the physical, economic, and natural resources of the state Assam. It also discussed at length, the various sectors of the economy and their present state of development. Important areas covered are development of decentralised sector, small scale industries, economic planning and problem of unemployment etc., It also presents, a summary of the report of the Task Force on Economic development of Assam, the Industrial Policy of Assam, the importance and the role of agro-based industry and banking sector in Assam. At the end author suggests an action plan for the optimal resource utilisation in a manner conducive to the over all development of the state.

Dutta and Karna (1987) edited a book on land relations in North East India. This book is the outcome of research papers presented in a seminar on 'land and land relations in the Hills of north east India' in May 1981 at Shillong. The book contains twenty five articles, in all, out of which four are of general category, one on Assam, two on Manipur, ten on Meghalaya, two on Mizoram and three each on Nagaland and Tripura. The book is a good account of issues related to inequality, poverty and changing social and agrarian relations in north east India.

Saha (1987) analyses the prevailing land systems in the tribal areas, along with various other issues like population density, distributional operational holdings, occupational strucutre and use of technology in agricultural sector. Author expresses its serious concern of emerging of the process of private ownership of land in tribal areas, which may breed to social conflicts through development of hierarchy in society, in long run. He opined that social management of land, based on collective and co-operative farming will serve the interest of the tribal people better.

An empirical study of agricultural and non-agricultural land use in Assam, along with inter state comparison is available in Goswami (1988). Author made a case for more effective implementation of regulation and acts related to land reforms in the state for faster and proper socio-economic justice.

Siddiqui (1990) presents a book on evolution of land grants and labour policies of the government and its impact on the growth of tea industry in Assam for the period 1834 to 1940. According to author, the successful growth of tea industry during this period has largely been dependent on two factors: (I) availability of land and (ii) adequate supply of labour.

Other factors which contributed to the growth of the industry such as transport, capital, market and management have not been examined in this study. The main line of argument through out the book is that the development of the tea industry was possible only at enormous social and economic cost to the local people of Assam. Study follows a traditional economic historian approach and relies heavy on the compilation of various historical time series data to substantiate the major findings and conclusions.

References

Adhikari, O.S. (1986), "A Simple Theoretical Approach to the Problem of Land Alienation", in Dutta, B.B. (ed.), Gagan Publishers, Ludhiana, 106–114.

Agarwal, A.K. (1986),"Changing Pattern of Agrarian relation in Arunachal Pradesh", in Dutta, B.B. (ed.), Gagan Publishers, Ludhiana, 175–182.

Bora, A.K. (1986), *Pattern of Land Utilisation in Assam,* Manas Publications, Delhi.

Dutta, B.B. (1986) (ed.), *Land use Pattern in North East India,* Gagan Publishers, Ludhiana.

Dutta, B.B. and Karna, M.N. (1987) (eds.), *Land Relations in North East India,* People's Publishing House, New Delhi.

Goswami, A. (1986) (ed.), *Land Reforms and Peasant Movement,* Omsons Publications, New Delhi.

Goswami, P.C. (1988), "Land Utilisation and its Economic Implications with Special Reference to Assam", in Thakur, P. (ed.), *Profile of a Development Strategy for India's North East,* Span Publications Pvt. Ltd., Guwahati, 24–34.

Mali, D.D. (1989), *Economic Problems and Planning in Assam,* Omsons Publications, Guwahati.

Neog, A.K. and Bordoloi, B. (1986), "Distributive Pattern of Land Holdings and Planned Agricultural Development in North Eastern Region of India", in Dutta, B.B. (ed.), Gagan Publishers, Ludhiana, 18–30.

Saha, N. (1987), "Land Systems and Agricultural Development in the Hills of North Eastern Region", in Dutta, B.B. and Karna, M.N. (eds.), People's Publishing House, New Delhi, 20–29.

Siddique, Muhammad Abu, B. (1990), *Evolutions of Land Grants and Labour Policies of Government: The Growth of Tea Industry in Assam 1834–1940,* South Asian Publishers, New Delhi.

Sinha, A.C. (1984). "Managing Social Consequences of Smallness: The Developmental Strategies for the Small Indian Frontier States", in Abbi, B.L. (ed.), *North Eastern Region: Problems and Prospects of Development,* Centre for Research in Rural and Industrial Development, Chandigarh, 111–123.

IV

ECONOMIC SYSTEM

Economic system is an organisation in which the economic activities take place among the economic agents. An efficient economic system ensures the fulfilment of economic interests of the economic agents. To understand the nature and functioning of an economic organisation, one has to study the characteristics of the people and society of a region. Some studies are also available in north-east where such attempts have been made, which give a clear picture of the prevailing economic systems, their functions and major changes which are taking place due to impacts of inter and intra regional developmental activities.

A study on the economy of Karbi Anglong is presented by Holloi (1978). It is a statistical analysis of the socio-economic structure of Karbi-Anglong. The author has collected the data from the publications of the Directorate of Economics & statistics, Government of Assam since 1951 and presented a comprehensive analysis which is quite useful for the researchers.

Goswami (1971) edited a volume on socio-economic research in tribal areas. Research articles are arranged in three sections: (i) social factors affecting economic development; (ii) problems of field investigation in tribal areas; (iii) village study as a tool of socio-economic research in tribal areas. Most of the papers have the developmental problems in the tribal areas as their focus.

In pioneering attempt Mali (1979) presents an introductory book on the economy of Meghalaya. This book contains fifteen chapters covering the various aspects of the economy of Meghalaya, like availability of mineral and forest resources, population, agriculture, land tenure systems, industries, community development and economic planning of the state. The emergence of North East council and its role in the economic development of the state is also highlighted.

Jha (1985) made an attempt to study the role of economic, social and organisational factors in the economic development of the state Arunachal Pradesh. The book is comprised of five units. The first unit is devoted to the basic structure of the hill economy of Arunachal Pradesh. In this part availability of natural resources, population base and the socio-economic fabric of the tribal people, have been discussed at length. Second unit deals with the status of agriculture, horticulture, marketing facilities, and various community-based services in the state. Industrial sector is incorporated in unit three while unit four is devoted to services sector. Last unit contains the status of economic development and economic planning in the state.

A village level empirical study is available with Ansari (1986) on socio-economic development of the tribal areas of Manipur. This study is about the Nungsai village in Manipur. It was observed by the author, that hilly village has limited resources but has benefited by inter regional links and contains with the Meiteis in the valley. The author suggests that this agriculture based village should improve its quality of agriculture for its socio-economoic development.

Ahluwalia (1986) edited a volume on social and economic development in North East India. This volume is a collection of articles dealing with various developmental issues concerning the region. The major issues covered by the researchers in their contribution to the volume are agriculture, manpower, transport, energy, tourism, along with role of North-Eastern Council has also been discussed.

Das (1986) studied the socio-economic status of scheduled caste of Assam. This study describes the origin of scheduled castes in Assam and views them in the wider context of the Indian caste system. The author has also highlighted the various economic and administrative measures taken by the state to uplift the status of these under privileged class.

Samanta (1987) analyses the economic system and social organisation of tribals, where community is governed by its own social codes and conducts which regulate the social life at large. While discussing to tribal development, policy and strategy, it is important and relevant to borne in mind that the different tribal communities are at different levels of socio-economic development. Author also emphasises the need to develop proper economic and administration institutions for example, there is a need to develop an institution which accounts the land records for the tribals in order to avoid the losts of land through alienation and lack of awareness.

Guhathakurta (1986) presents an economic and ethnographic account of the people of Tripura. The author has also discussed various problems faced by the society due to sudden increase in the population in 1950s, its peculiar geographical location, lack of infrastructural facilities, unemployment etc.

In an empirical study Nair (1987) made an attempt to capture the relevant economic contemporary issues of the state Meghalaya. In an inter-temporal analysis, based on extensive field survey, author ascertains the major changes in land tenure system, pattern of its distribution and use. Description is also available on organisation of labour, production and consumption patterns. The issues related to transition from shifting to settled cultivation in East Khasi Hills are also discussed.

Jha (1988) analyses the socio-economic and demographic dimensions of Arunachal Pradesh, which covers a vast range of issues concerning the organisation of agriculture and related economic activities, problems of industrialisation, unemployment and demographic features etc. This volume is a collection of articles on diverse topics such as land tenure system, agrarian structure, extent of practising shifting cultivation and socio-economic changes in the Arunachal society. The author suggests the appropriate technology, the basis of techno-structure, suitable to socio-economic and environmental dimensions of the region has to be looked into and applied. It is emphasised that technology is a powerful and effective devise through which the life and living standards of the people of the region may be improved.

Payeng (1988) focusses attention on the economic and social changes in some tribal groups of Arunachal Pradesh. Based on secondary source material this volume attempts to explain the distinctive characteristic features of tribes. The author maintains that the various reform measures have created conflicts in the way of life of these societies.

Bhattacharjee (1989) edited a volume which is a collection of articles presented in a seminar on the sequences of development in North-East India. The articles touch upon the various aspects of rural development, developmental programs, planning, social change and processes of modernisation etc. A large number of articles deal with the north-eastern scenario in general, but there are some articles dealing with specific area of the region or specific issues e.g., education, employment, etc.

Upadhaya (1989) presents a systematic study based on primary data to analyse the production structure and consumption -expenditure pattern of a hilly tribal village of the state Mizoram. The objective of the economic survey of the Dungdai village of the Aizawl district, has been to assess the viability of the economy with the prevailing production relations and income generation distribution pattern. A useful statistic is collected, tabulated to analyse the issues such as occupational pattern, saving and investment potential, housing and level of poverty in the village.

In a well organised study Islam (1989) presents a critical analysis of the transition of Nagaland's economy from a primitive to a modern economy. This book contains nine chapters and deals mainly with the intersectoral analysis of the state economy. The issues related to economic development during third, fourth, fifth and sixth five year plans are also discussed at length. It is concluded that the pace of development in Nagaland's economy is relatively slow in the region. While Indian economy has entered the take-off stage. The economy of Nagaland had only achieved the precondition stage for 'take-off, till the beginning of sixth five year plan.

References

Ahluwalia, S. (ed.), *Social and Economic Development in North-East India*, Gian Publishing House, Delhi.

Ansari, S.A. (1986), *Socio-Economic Development in Tribal Areas of Manipur*, B.R. Publishing Corporation, Delhi.

Bhattacharjee, J.B. (1989) (ed.), *Sequences of Development in North-East India*, Omsons Publications, Guwahati,, Delhi.

Das, Bhakta (1986), *A Glimpse of the Scheduled Castes and their Socio-Economic Development in Assam*, Omsons Publications, Guwahati.

Gogoi, Pradip Kumar (1978), *The Economy of Karbi-Anglong*, Gauhati, Directorate of Economics and Statistics, Government of Assam, 1978.

Goswami, P.C. (1971), "Socio-Economic Research in Tribal Areas", *Agro-Economic Research Centre for North-East India*, Jorhat, Assam, 1971.

Guhathakurta, S.N. (1986), *Tripura*, National Book Trust, New Delhi.

Islam, Saleh Swabera (1989), *Nagaland's Economy in Transition Since 1964*, Omsons Publications, Delhi.

Jha, S.D. (1985), *The Wealth of Arunachal Pradesh*, Mittal Publications, Delhi.

Jha, S.D. (1988), *Socio-Economic and Demographic Dimensions of Arunachal Pradesh*, Omsons Publications, Guwahati.

Mali, D.D. (1978), *An Introduction to the Economy of Meghalaya*, Ratna Mascot, Shillong.

Nair, M.K.S. (1987), *Tribal Economy in Transition: A Study of Meghalaya*, Inter-India Publications, Delhi.

Payeng, H. (1988), *Economic & Social Change in North-East*, Criterion Publications, New Delhi.

Samanta, R.K. (1987), "Landless Tribal People and Basic Needs for their Development"' in Dutta B.B. and M.N, Karna, *Land Relations in North-East India*, People's Publishing House, New Delhi, 30–39.

Upadhyaya, K.K. (1989), *Semi Primitive Economy of an Indian Village*, Mittal Publications, Delhi.

V

ECONOMIC PLANNING

Economic planning was adopted as an instrument of development after India's independence. The principal Objectives of economic planning have been to achieve economic growth, self reliance and social justice. A number of steps were taken in north east India also during various Five Year Plans to boost the pace of economic development. Now when almost half century has passed since we have adopted plan regime, it is high time to evaluate critically the performance of developmental projects during plan. A number of studies tackle the micro and macro level planning, their implementation impacts and critical evaluation in the north eastern region are discussed below.

Singh (1980) worked on urban land use planning in hill areas. This work has been included because it describe certain aspects of the empirical reality which would be useful to the studies in economic planning. Especially, in the field of spatial planning in urban regions. In this context this work throws light on the demographic structure of the population, the patterns of residential, commercial and other forms of land use. Describing the urban front of Shillong the author also discusses the issues related to regional planning.

Guhathakurta (1982) studied some aspects of urbanisation in north-eastern region of India. Author analyses the decennial percentage growth of urban rural population in the region on the basis of population statistics published in 1981 census of India. The functional classification of the major towns, as manufacturing towns, trade and transport towns and service towns, is available in this study. It is observed that towns are growing in size and importance with a noticeable shift in the employment pattern from service sector to trade-transport and manufacturing sectors. Author suggests for a viable market potential study on regional basis for an efficient transport system for a systematic town planning.

The studies concerning work participation and occupational structure in a region clearly reflect the economic character of population. But, studies on north-eastern region on this line are very limited in number. However, in a pioneering work, Goel (1983) analysed the changing characteristics of the urban male work force in the North-East India during 1961–71, at district level by applying principal component analysis. The findings of the study indicate that the slow process of urbanisation in the region during the period did not result in any pronounced occupational change and diversity in the secondary activities.

Pakem (1984) edited a volume on the development of city Shillong during a decade 1971–81. This volume is a collection of papers presented in a symposium on the same theme organised by the North-East India Council for Social Science Research, Shillong in 1981. Divided into five sections, this book discusses various aspects of this cosmopolitan town. The contributors have described the administrative, political, economic, cultural and educational profile of the city.

Alam (1985a) presents a book, which is a collection of articles presented in the seminar held on "Planning in North-East India: Retrospective and Perspective", at Shillong in 1983 organised by the North-East India Council for Social Science Research, Shillong. This edited volume contains articles dealing six broad themes namely, national and regional planning process, social dimensions of planning, levels of planning: state and union territory, review and perspective of growth in north-east India, North east council and regional planning and strategies for long term planning and development. The book contains thirty-one articles relating to the diversified fields of development planning of the regional economies. In addition Alam (1985,b) also, edited a volume of research articles on the conceptual frame work of regional development and micro level planning. Articles contributed by the region's eminent economists, adminstrators, policy makers and other social scientists dealing with various aspects of regional planning like regional and specific development strategy, human resource development, regional planning, intersectoral inter regional co-ordination and integration, role of externalities and economies of scale and application of input-output techniques for the material balance model for the north eastern region. Alam (1985,c), discussed various instruments of planning in order to accelerate the pace of development of the region. For this purpose, author suggests a thorough reorganisation of the structure of planning. To ensure the social justice, grass root planning in the form of micro-level planning has been advocated, the public participation in plan formulation and implementation at the grass root level.

Barthakur (1985) emphasises that regional economies should plan for the effective utilisation of locally available resources in the primary and secondary sectors activities, based on a perspective man-power planning. In regard to the man-power development, it is stressed that in addition to job training for skill formation, there is also, a need for attitudinal and management training and orientation of educational system to raise the competitive ability of the people.

Mitra (1986,a) makes a critical analysis of the forestry planning during the five year plans in North-East India. It reveals that although there is a rapid increase in plan allocations in the forestry sector but the percentage allocation to total investment has reduced significantly. At the same time, the growth rate of revenue is more than that of plan allocations, which implies the increased rate of exploitation of forest resources of the region.

Deka (1986) analysed the issues related to spatial and temporal patterns of urbanisation in north eastern part of India for twenty years from 1961–81. The trends show the significant increase in population concentration in major urban centres in a heterogeneous manner in the region.

Trends and pattern of urbanisation in Arunachal Pradesh from 1971–81, is available in a study presented by Mitra (1986,b). It is observed that the process of urbanisation in this state is induced one i.e., it has been linked with the setting up of administrative headquarters at different levels. It is further noticed that inter-state migration has played an important role in explaining the urbanisation process in the region.

Duttaray (1987) presents a volume, which is a collection of research papers contributed to a three-day-workshop on

North-East India 2000 AD: Perspective for futurology, organised by North-East India Council for Social Science Research in April 1986 at Shillong. Volume contains twenty papers on diverse fields and aspects related to north-eastern economy. Besides economists, the renounced anthropologists, sociologists, demographers have also, contributed papers to this volume. Book also covers some of futurogical studies related to population, human settlement pattern, physical resources, scientific and technological developments, planning management, industrialisation, urbanisation, cultural resources, and institutional framework of north eastern area.

Agarwal (1987) meticulously discussed the regional economies of all the seven states of north-east India in a systematic manner. This book is divided into five parts, namely structure of regional economies, planning and economic development, basic issues in agriculture, industrial development and problems of banking sector in north-east. The study is based on voluminous secondary data collected and compiled from a number of sources. Book is useful for the students, who are interested in knowing the basic economic conditions and status of the north eastern states of India.

Sarma and Bhorali (1988) made an attempt to study the impact of planning on the economy of north-east. Authors have tried to find out the causes responsible for less effective implementation of planning in the region. It was pointed out that neglect of human resources, absence of grass root planning, slow process of industrialisation, and lack of political will are the main reasons for the partial success in planning.

Bordoloi (1988) studied the process of industrialisation in the region during five year plans. Author is of the view, that economic growth has a natural tendency towards polarisation, concentrating at certain points in space and from there to spread gradually towards other areas. So, as the industries also have the tendency of agglomerating in a few prosperous points. The process of agglomeration if not timely and properly countered, tends to be self sustaining and self-accentuating, pushing thereby the backward regions into a vicious circle. The north eastern regions of India, are not sharing equally the economic development process, which is evident by the fact that even today the entire north-eastern region barring three tea-growing districts of Assam remains, industrially backward. Author identifies the reasons responsible for this situation and opined that the region's industrial backwardness is characterised by the predominance of extractive industries having marginal local multiplier and linkage effect followed by absence of heavy capital goods industries. Modern ancillary industries are still in its infant stage. To come out of this situation an outline and framework of alternative regional planning system is discussed in detail.

Bhattacharya (1988) edits a volume on problems of urban development and planning in Guwahati. This book is an outcome of research papers presented to a seminar on "Save Guwahati" held in January, 1987. Articles published in the book deal with the various problems of a growing city, Guwahati, such as road accident proneness, drainage, water logging and sanitation problems, growing need of educational, medical and health facilities. Need was also felt for a detailed master plan of the city and its sincere implementation. Book highlights the short term and long term remedial measures for the betterment of the city.

The volume edited by Bhorali (1988) is the outcome of collected papers presented in a seminar on the impact of the five year plans on socio-economic growth of the north-eastern region of India, in January 1982. This seminar was organised by the Department of Economics, Guwahati University, Guwahati. In all, the volume contains thirty-four papers from diverse fields like, economic planning management, banking, trade and commerce, transport and agricultural development. Some papers also provide statistical analysis and empirical evidences to highlight the impact of five year plans on the socio-economic life of the people of the region. Some authors have also discussed the major weaknesses of planning process and proposed some measures to improve the implementation of planning in a more effective way to fulfil the long cherished goal of balanced and self sustained economic growth of region. The book lacks the editor's remarks and contribution in organising the papers properly, theme-wise in a systematic manner.

Pathak (1988) put forward some concrete suggestions, by way of a development strategy for the region. Author finds this region as an interesting case for experimenting with regional development techniques, research and formulation of development programs. It also opens up a scope for research in the field of resource analysis, the exploitation and location of various types of economic activities. Author stressed that a viable development strategy for the region must be concentrated on human resource and infrastructural development; forests and mineral based industries and urban industrial growth. In this process author calls for the vital role of North-Eastern Council for regional balanced economic development.

A viable regional development planning requires a strong database and the applications of various techniques of regional analysis. Sarma (1988) identifies the types and areas in which the attention should be paid on priority basis, to collect and compile the necessary data at desegregated level such as human resource availability, inter- and intra-regional migration, regional social accounting containing inter regional trade flows commodity wise, in and out flow statistics and comparative cost analysis. Author also, suggests some appropriate approaches could be applied for regional planning by developing a model on the lines of industrial complex approach, raw material planning, growth centre strategy, cost-benefit analysis and quality control planning.

Mali (1989) presents a book on the various economic aspects of the state Assam. This book contains eighteen chapters dealing with economic resources, development of agriculture, land reforms, small- and large-scale industries, transport sector, state domestic products, revenue and expenditure analysis and economic planning. Economic problems like unemployment and price movements have also got place in the book. It also contains rich bibliography and a systematic indexing at the end. The scope of the book is very wide which limits the author to do in-depth analysis of any aspect of the economy.

Agarwal (1989) reviewed the developmental achievements during the plan period in Arunachal Pradesh. It is observed that large amount of development expenditure is being made towards in construction and maintenance of public works. In the absence of industrial base state economy has very low backward linkage effects of planned expenditure. In fact development expenditure further distorting the income distribution in favour of higher income group people. Author emphasises of redefining the plan priorities, which are helpful in balanced regional development.

Das (1990) proposed a new paradigm of development to reduce the level of regional imbalance. The net per capita domestic product of India is compared with per capita state domestic product of Assam for the twenty-five years of planning. Author suggests that the objectives of maximising the output and employment should be given top priority while plan outlay is allocated among economic sectors. This would be possible when preference will be given to those sectors which use the locally available raw materials as input in the process of production.

Man power planning in the country like India is greatly influenced by market forces which are imperfect by nature. The prevailing practice of hiring and placement of labour reveals the skill requirement for specific occupation and availability of skill in the market. Any deviation from between the required qualification and actually possessed by those who are recruited is a reflection of the condition of labour market. Lawma (1990) made an attempt to analyse this dimension of the manpower planning process in the north-east region of India. It was observed that besides the minimum qualification the job training, technical education, work experience in general play an important role in job entry.

References

Agarwal, A.K. (1987), *Economic Problems and Planning in North-East India*, Sterling Publishers Private Limited, New Delhi.

Alam, Khorshed (1985a) (ed.), *Planning in North-East India*, Omsons Publications, Guwahati.

Alam, Khorshed (1985b) (ed.), *Regional Development and Microlevel Planning: A Conceptual Framework*, Omsons Publications, New Delhi.

Alam, Khorshed, (1985c), "Planning in North-East India" in Alam (ed.), *Regional Development and Microlevel Planning: A Conceptual Framework*, Omsons Publications, New Delhi, 20–32.

Barthakur (1985),"Development of Human Resources for Agricultural and Allied Sectors in the North-East Hill Region", in Alam (1985b), Omsons Publications, New Delhi, 33–46.

Bhattacharya, B.K. (1988) (ed.), *Problems of Urban Development in Guwahati*, Omsons Publications, New Delhi.

Bhorali, D. (1988) (ed.), *Economic Development of North Eastern Region*, Spectrum Publications, Guwahati.

Bordoloi, Gopal (1988), "Five Year Plans and Industrialisation in North-Eastern Region of India", in Bhorali, D. (ed.), Spectrum Publications, Guwahati, 215–223.

Das, H.N. (1990), "A New Paradigm of Development: Regional Imbalances in Assam", in Barua, P.C. (ed.), *Development Planning of North-East India*, Mittal Publications, New Delhi, 149–160.

Deka, P. (1986)," Spatial and Temporal Urbanisation in North-East India, 1961–81", *Indian Journal of Regional Science*, Vol. XVIII, No.-1, 17–24.

Dutta Ray, B. (1987) (ed.), *North-East India 2000 A.D.: Perspective for Futurology*, Deep & Deep Publications, New Delhi.

Goel, N.P. (1983), "Change in the Characteristics of Urban Male Work Force in North-East India, 1961–1971: A Statistical Analysis", *Hill Géographer*, Vol. 2, No. 2, 22–25.

Guhathakurta, S.N. (1982), "Some Aspects of Urbanisation in North-Eastern Region of India: A Preliminary Note". *The Journal of North-East Indian Council for Social Science Research*, April, Vol. 4, No.-1, 1–9.

Lawma, T. (1990), *Market Imperfection and Manpower Planning*, Commonwealth Publishers, New Delhi.

Mali, D.D. (1989), *Economic Problems and Planning in Assam*, Omsons Publications, New Delhi.

Mitra, Amitav (1986a),"An Assessment of Forestry Planning in North-East India During Five Year Plans", in M. Dasgupta et. al. (eds.), *Forestry Development in North-East India*, Omsons Publications, New Delhi, 126–134.

Mitra, Amitva, (1986b),"Trends and Pattern of Urbanisation in Arunachal Pradesh, 1971–81", in Ganguli, J.B. (ed.), *Urbanisation and Development in North-East India*, Deep & Deep Publications, New Delhi, 147–153.

Pakem, B. (1984) (ed.), *Shillong: 1971–81*, Research India Publications, Calcutta.

Pathak, C.R. (1988),"Development Strategy for North-East Region, Some Suggestions" in Thakur, Pankaj (ed.), *Profile of Development Strategy for India's North-East*, Span Publications, Pvt. Ltd., Guwahati, 111–119.

Sarma, Anil Kumar and Devdas Bhorali (1988), "Impact of Planning on the North-Eastern Economy: A case study of Soaring Ideology and Grim Reality" in Bhorali, D. (ed.) *Economic Development of North-Eastern Region*, Spectrum Publications, Guwahati, 9–20.

Sarma, P. (1988), "Development of the North-East Region: Some Missing Dimensions in the Current Strategy" in Thakur Pankaj (ed.), Span Publications, Guwahati, 3–23.

Singh, J.P. (1980), *Urban Land Use Planning in Hill Areas: A Case Study of Shillong*, Inter India Publications, Delhi.

VI

ECONOMIC DEVELOPMENT

The Economics of Development is a subject branch of Economics, dealing with the problems of economic development of a developing region. The term 'economic development' is generally used in many other synonymous terms such as economic growth, economic welfare, secular change, social justice and economic progress. Underdeveloped economies are normally characterised by excessive dependency on agriculture, low per capita income, dualism, high growth of population, unemployment, slow and unbalanced industrial growth, and lack of entrepreneurial ability. By and large, most of these characteristics are also depicts by the regional economies of north east India. The issues related to economic development, the region has attracted the attention of the economists to a large extent, which is available in the form of published research work in the region.

Goswami & Saikia (1971) studied the status of economic development in the tribal areas of North Eastern Frontier Area (NEFA). The three factors are chosen as main determinants of economic growth in hill areas, namely, development of local marketing centres, desires to save and invest and opportunities for investment. The number of socio-economic issues are identified which are responsible for slow economic growth. It is suggested that prevailing attitude will have to be modified by interacting with outside world and consequent awareness of the necessity of better standard of living. For self sustaining economic growth local production system must be improved through easy means of transport, marketing and new techniques of production.

Ganguli (1974) analyses the problems and prospect of economic development of the state Tripura. Author stressed on issues like population pressure and land use pattern by utilising the statistics on population density, growth and nubmer of operational holdings in different size classes. It is observed that the problem of unemployment is growing alarmingly which needs to address immediately. More intense efforts in the fifth five year plan was called for the balanced industrial development of the state.

Khaund (1976) introduces the functions of North-Eastern Council (NEC). The basic objective of the insitute is to operate as an instrument for economic integration of the region through harmonious process of socio-economic development. Attempt is made in this study to evaluate the role of NEC in achieving it's objectives, critically since its inception.

Abbi (1984) edited a volume of collected articles, which is the outcome of the research papers presented to a seminar held in April 1981, undertaken by the Centre for Research in Rural and Industrial Development, Chandigarh. The Volume contains four parts, including various inter disciplinary themes, like economic development and social tensions, social and cultural diversity and quest for national integration, Assam movement identities and influx of foreigners, etc. However, the students of economics would be interested more in part II of the book, which deals with demographic transformation in the context of influx of migrants, inadequate and unbalanced economic development and its causes and remedial measures.

Alagh and Goswami (1984) discuss the details of a development strategy for Assam. Authors have identified four main reasons for low level of industrialisation: (i) small market, (ii) lack of enterpreneurship, (iii) poor infrastructure and (iv) high transport cost. Keeping these factors in mind, study suggests the remedial measures, such as development of road and rail transport network, larger public investment and development of locally available resource based industries.

Ganguli (1984) draws the attention towards the peculiarities of North-Eastern region vis-a-vis of the other parts of India. Because of regional and social specificities, one has to be more careful in planning development strategy for the region. Author emphasises that strategy should pay more attention to area planning, optimising the use of locally available resources and labour. This would need to evolve an economic management system which ensures people's active participation in the decision-making and implementing process.

Sinha (1984) establishes the relationship of development strategy with the size of state in the context of north eastern region. The size of the state is affected by the various factors like ecological, ethnic, economic, political status of the region. The development strategy which is suitable for bigger size states can't be applicable for the small size states. Author suggests that the analytical frame work and problems of smaller states can be understood in terms of; resource availability, interstate linkages, regional perspective and expectation from the centre and high rate of immigration.

In the present work Upadhyaya (1985) brings out the main considerations in planning a development strategy for the state Mizoram. Author visualises some crucial parameters of the state economy and studies the emerging production relation in primary sector and the prospects of the development of agro-based industries. It is observed that Mizoram is rich in water and forest resources. So, it has great potential in commercial production of forest products like rubber, coffee, tea and pine. The environment is very conducive for cattle farming and dairy development.

Somayajulu (1985) analyses the structure of the economy of Meghalaya. It also examines the consumer behaviour of households in rural and urban sectors in terms of expenditure elasticities of different items of consumption classifying them into necessities, semi luxuries and luxuries. Author suggests a development strategy based on agricultural and agro-based industries for the state Meghalaya.

Goswami (1985) deals with the review of patterns of economic growth in north-east India. Author stressed on the need of a clear enunciation of the contents of economic development suitable in the regional context. For example industrial development per se is not economic development; it promotes economic development only when it leads to the formation of local skill, radiates growth stimulus for further investment by raising labour productivity, income, capital formation and creation of externalities with proper economies of scale. Author suggests to develop an appropriate industrial policy for the region, keeping long term perspective in mind.

Dutta (1985) put forward the view that the social restlessness of people of the region hampering the required peaceful situation for industrial and economic development. Further, author opined that as long as the policy makers at the centre continue to be the victim of war-psychoses and haunted by the concept of border state, it will be difficult to over come the inertia as the status of economic development in the region would remain gloomy. Baruah (1985) proposed to treat North-Eastern Region as an economic unit which should follow a strategy of unbalanced growth in short run, though the long term strategy should be a balanced, self sufficient and self sustained growth. This study is based on an application of Input-Output co-effeicient matrix for Assam, assuming it as a representative input-output coefficient matrix for the north-eastern region.

On the basis of linkage analysis it is observed that resource allocation during five year plan is not done judiciously. For example the industrial and mineral sector which has significantly higher linkage effect is not given proper weightage as only about 5 per cent of the total plans outlay allocated to these sectors. It is further suggested that since the planning machineries of the constituent units of the region frame their plans independently, the North-Eastern Council is expected to act as a co-ordinator in bringing out a common strategy of development for the region.

To deal with problems of economic development due to land alienation among the tribals of Tripura, Dasgupta (1987) developed a mathematical model based on the model earlier developed by Hirschman (1978) to study the changing tolerance for income inequality in the course of economic development. In this paper author tries to explain the relations of the tribal to land alienation, to fellow tribals and to non-tribals. Present model is static, as claimed by the author herself, needs an extension to explain the dynamic situation with empirical testing of the hypotheses.

For the past three decades the Government of India has been devoting its special attention for the quick economic development and all round advancement of North-Eastern Region. It is imperative on the part of scholars and academicians to study the emerging trends as consequence of such development. In one such efforts Mahajan (1987) brings together a collection of research papers contributed by the economists dealing with the variety of areas of regional development. This edited volume contains nineteen papers arranged in two parts, where part I deals with macro aspect and part II deals the micro dimensions of the regional economies.

Sri Prakash (1987) makes an in-depth analysis of the various aspects of economic growth in the region and in particular draws attention on the prevailing wide income disparities among the different units of the region. Author adds that despite higher growth rate in State Domestic Products (SDP) in the region compared with national level growth in Gross Domestic Products (GDP) the effect of higher investment in the former has been far lower. Such situation coupled with high population and consumer prices growth had entrenched this area in a low equilibrium trap.

Sen (1987) in his study analyses the consumption pattern of the region. The author concludes that expenditure on food in rural area is proportionately higher than in urban area. In recent years there has been a downward trend in such expenditure which is the consequence of rise of income due to industrialisation in rest of India, but such an effect is not visible in case of North East India. This study is based on consumer expenditure data published by National Sample Survey, time to time.

Upadhyaya (1987) worked on an alternate model of development for the state Mizoram. For the purpose of analysis author divides the post independence period into three distinct periods and elaborate the changes in the socio-economic structure under each period. The author suggests that for encouraging orderly growth and better income and asset distribution the subsidies which have mainly benefited only a few, individual should be withdrawn in a systematic and phased manner.

It is a great concern for social scientists that even after the fifty years of planning the economic distance between north-eastern region and the rest of India is continuously increasing. The economic under-development is total, covering the all major areas like agriculture, irrigation, power, transport, industry, and human resource development. The situation demands for serious re-appraisal of prevailing development approaches. To fill this gap a critical evaluation of regional development strategy is available in Thakur (1988), an edited volume which is published in the honour of Prof. Parmeswar Sarma, a well known economist of Assam. The book contains eleven articles on the development policy related to various economic sectors like land, agriculture, power, transport, irrigation and industry of Assam. Author suggests that region specific micro level development strategy should be adopted instead of a uniform approach to economic development for all under-developed areas of the region.

Sharma (1988) discussed power development strategy in relation to the hydel power potentials and utilisation prospects of the region. Study also presents the regional breakups of power potential and the techno-economic feasible schemes that can be taken up. The prospects and possibilities of natural gas-based power plants are also discussed keeping in mind the availability of oil and natural gas resources in Assam.

Bhorali (1988) edited a volume on economic development of north-east region. This volume is an outcome of papers presented in a seminar on the impact of the five year plans on the socio-economic growth of the region. This seminar was organised by the department of commerce, Gauhati University in January 1982. This book contains thirty four papers dealing with impact of planning on rural infrastructural, agricultural and industrial development of the states of NER. Some papers highlighted the role of institutional sectors like banks, planning administration and public sector in the areas of economic development. Need was also felt by Goswami (1988) to establish and develop a research training institute to study the regional aspects of economic develpment and social change in NE India.

Mahajan (1988) edited a volume of research articles on the economic development of the region. Book contains the articles contributed by a number of economists and other social scientists of the region. These articles cover varied fields of economic development like regional planning, evaluation of rural development, status of agricultural and industrial sector, efficiency of infrastructural sector and develpment of region specific strategy to deal with the peculiar socio-ecnomic problems. In the same volume Mahajan (1988a) studied the constraints of agricultural development in Mizoram. This is based on a policy paper prepared by the author, which suggests a fifteen year long term plan to convert the shifting cultivation into settled cultivation. Author has also worked out in detail the precondition for the success of such program and total resources involved in this exercise.

Agarwal (1988) presents a monograph on problems and prospects of North-Eastern Economy; based on secondary source materials. In the background of varying problems in planning for the development, the author attempts to examine the various issues involving the economic development of the region. The book contains twelve chapters dealing with infrastructure, problems of unemployment and migration, regional planning and role of North-Eastern Council in the development of agriculture and small scale industrial sector. The author has also suggested approaches and remedial measures to deal with the economic problems of the region.

Bhattacharjee (1989) edited a volume which is the outcome of research articles presented to a seminar on Sequences of Development in North-East India held in December 1985, organised by North-East India Council for Social Science Research in Shillong. This volume is a collection of twenty five articles contributed by prominent social scientists of the region. Most of the scholars discussed the economic, social, cultural and political aspects of developmental changes which have been taking place among the tribal communities of North-Eastern India.

Guhathakurta (1989) examined the relationship between unemployment and poverty based on a field study in Meghalaya. Field situation relates to hilly areas where land man ratio is high, so it is difficult to ascertain the unemployment level with the help of conventional conceptual tools. The element of wage labour was found to be negligible but the practice of reciprocal labour without involving any cash transaction still exists. The incidence of poverty is more acute than incidence of unemployment. Findings of the study suggests that labour productivity is low in hilly areas and hence, poverty exists despite of employment.

Saikia (1989) examined the role of women in agricultural sector of Assam and found that except when driven by acute economic hardship females in this region, by and large, don't go for wage employment. They mostly work in their own farms. The average employment of female labour for marginal, small and medium farmers in days per hectare of gross cropped area is found to be very low. Similarly, the extent of utilisation of female labour as proportion to total working days available in farm work in one year is also very low. This suggests that the contribution of female workers in agricultural production depends on sex division of work. It is recommended for rational utilisation of female labour force by developing skill and imparting education.

Ganguli (1989) has made an attempt to study the process of diversification and specialisation of productive activities of tribal villages in region in the context of a new structure of social-economic and political relations based on private ownership of property and stratification of society in to different economic groups. Author highlights the emergence of peasant farmers class, their income structure and role in village economy.

Barua (1990) edits a volume of collection of research papers contributed by eminent social scientists at various seminars organised during 1985–87, jointly by North-East Institute of Bank Management and Guwahati Management Association, Assam. The volume is comprised of four units containing paper related to Ecology and land use, approach to development of the region, rural and man power development. In all, there are thirty-six articles in this volume, covers a wide range of subjects, which aims at evolving a co-ordinated and integrated strategy for optimum and 'just' development of the region.

Rai et al (1990) edit a volume on the issues related to hill area development. This volume is an outcome of papers presented by various social scientists in a seminar on Problems of Hill Area Development, held at Shillong in 1988. Book contains twenty-nine articles which are organised in four sections. The first section is devoted to papers related to general theoretical context of developmental issues and their applicability in the regional context. The issues related to environmental basis of development in the hills region are dealt in section II. The section III of the book emphasises on the position of agricultural development in hills, whereas, section IV deals with the role and status of infrastructural factors in the development of the hill areas.

References

Abbi, B.L. (1984) (ed.), *North-Eastern Region: Problems and Prospects of Development*, Centre for Research in Rural and Industrial Development, Chandigarh.

Agrawal A.K. (1988), *North-East Economy: Problems and Prospects*, Mittal Publications, Delhi.

Alagh Y.K. and Goswami, Atul (1984), "Some Issues of Development Strategy for Assam", in Abbi, B.L. (eds.), Centre for Research in Rural and Industrial Development, Chandigarh.

Alagh, Y.K. and Sharma P.S. (1980), "Growth of Crop Production: Is it Decelerating?", *Indian Journal of Agricultural Economics*, April 104–118.

Barua, P.C. (1990) (ed.), *Development Planning of North-East India*, Mittal Publications, New Delhi.

Barua, Sri Nath (1985), "Certain Observations on the Strategy of Development of the North-Eastern Region", in Alam, K. (ed.), *Regional Development and Micro Level Planning: A Conceptual Frame Work*, Omsons Publications, New Delhi, 268–274.

Bhattacharjee, J.B. (1989) (ed.), *Sequences in Development of North-East India*, Omsons Publications,Guwahati.

Bhorali D. (1988) (ed.), *Economic Development of the North-Eastern Region*, Spectrum Publications, New Delhi.

Dasgutpa, Malabika (1987), "Land Alienation and Social Discontent in Tripura: A Preliminary Hypotheses", in Dutta, B.B. and Karna, M.N. (eds.), *Land Relations in North-East India*, People's Publishing House, New Delhi, 234–242.

Dutta, P.S. (1985), "Role of Socio-Economic Psychology in Industrial Development of North-East", *Journal of North-East India Council for Social Research*, Shillong, Vol. 9, No. 1, April, 31–36.

Ganguli, J.B. (1974), "Problems and Prospects of Economic Development of Tripura", *The North-East Research Bulltein*, V, Summer, 25–35.

Ganguli, J.B. (1984), "Development and Social Tension in North-Eastern Region", in Abbi, B.L. (eds.), Centre for Research in Rural and Industrial Development, Chandigarh, 99–110.

Ganguli, J.B. (1989), "Economic Development of the Tribal Villages of North-East India", in Bhattacharjee J.B. (ed.), Omsons Publications, Delhi, 41–55.

Goswami, Atul (1985), "Contents of Economic Development for North-East India", in Alam, K. (ed.), *Planning in North-East India*, Omsons Publications, New Delhi, 191–198.

Goswami, P.C. (1988), "Problems of Integrated Development of North-East India: Need of Research Centre for the Region", in Bhorali, D. (ed.), Spectrum Publications, Guwahati, 9–12.

Goswami, P.C. and Saikia, P.D. (1971), "Problems of Economic Development in Tribal Areas with Special Reference to Dafla and Gallong Tribes of NEFA", *The North-East Research Bulletin,* Vol. II Summer, 33–42.

Guhathakurta, S.N. (1989), "Relationship between Unemployment and Poverty: Some Tentative Hypotheses", in Saikia and Phukan (1989) (eds.), *Rural Development in North-East India,* D.K. Publishing and Distribution (p) Ltd., Delhi, 129–140.

Hirschman A.O. (1978), "The Changing Tolerance for Income Inequality in the Course of Economic Development", in S.P. Singh (ed.), *Under Development to Developing Economies,* Oxford University Press, 517–543.

Khaund, T.P. (1976), "Role of North Eastern Council in Economic Development in NE India", *The North East Research Bulletin,* VII, Summer, 30–35.

Mahajan, V.S. (1987) (ed.), *Emerging Pattern of North-Eastern Economy,* Deep & Deep Publication, New Delhi.

Mahajan, V.S. (1988a), "Development Strategy for Mizoram: An Exercise in its Long Term Growth Through Conversion of Shifting Cultivation in to Settled Land Use and Resources Involved There in", Mahajan (1988) (ed.), Deep & Deep Publications, Delhi.

Mahajan, V.S. (1988) (ed.), *Economic Development of Border States in India,* Deep & Deep Publications, Delhi.

Rai, R.K., Mohapatra A.C., Mishra S.K., Nayak, D.K., and Butola B.S. (1990) (eds.), *Hill Area Development: Issues and Perspectives,* Rawat Publications, Jaipur.

Saikia, A. (1989), "Role of Women in Agriculture in Assam", in Saikia and Phukan (1989) (ed.), D.K. Publishing and Distribution (P) Ltd., Delhi, 195–206.

Sen, R.K. (1987), "Consumption Pattern of North-East India", in Maharani, V.S. (ed.), Deep & Deep Publications, New Delhi, 80–95.

Sharma, P.C. (1988), "Power Development Strategy for North-East Region: Some Important Aspects", in Thakur P. (ed.), Span Publications Private Limited, Guwahati, 62–76.

Sinha, A.C. (1984), "Managing Social Consequences of Smallness: The Development Strategy for the Small Indian Frontier State", in Abbi, B.L. (ed.), Centre for Research in Rural and Industrial Development, Chandigarh, 111–123.

Somayajulu, V.V.N. (1985), "Development Strategy for Meghalaya, Income Distribution and Employment", *Journal of North-East India Council for Social Science Research,* April, Vol. IX, No. 1, 9–16.

Sri Prakash (1987), "Development of the Economy of North-East India: Current Status", in Maharani, V.S. (ed.), Deep & Deep Publications, New Delhi.

Thakur, Pankaj (1988) (ed.), *Profile of a Development Strategy for India's North-East,* Span Publications Private Limited, Guwahati.

Upadhyaya, K.K. (1985), *Development Problems and prospects of Mizoram: Tribal Studies of India,* Series: T 117, Inter India Publications, New Delhi.

Upadhyaya, K.K. (1987), "Alternate Model of Development for Mizoram", in Maharani, V.S. (ed.), Deep & Deep Publications, New Delhi, 256–263.

VII

INDUSTRIAL ECONOMICS

Rapid industrialisation can play a significant role in accelerating the rate of growth of an economy, but the process of industrialisation itself require, a number of socio-economic prerequisites. In the absence of favourable conditions the process of industrialisation would either be slow or unbalanced or both. In this situation state has to play a vital role, in the form of promoter, by way of direct and indirect participation in this process. In this direction Central Government has declared the entire north eastern region as an industrially backward and offers a number of incentives for rapid industrialisation.

As a matter of fact, region has a fairly long history of industrial activities and availability of required resource raw materials. During the British rule attempts were initiated to explore and exploit some of these resources. Among these, tea, coal and mineral oil industries are worth mentioning. In spite of this the region continues to be one of least developed region of India in terms of industrialisation. The industrial sector employ only 5.78 per cent of the region's total workforce as per 1991 census. The following section presents few research works dealing some of the relevant issues related to the region's industries.

Awasthi (1975) presents a work on the economics of tea industry in India, with special reference to Assam. This study is a detailed account of the growth and development of tea plantation and manufacture along with organisation, management, labour, finance, marketing, transport, price trends and export promotion activities of tea industry in Assam. Almost all the economic aspects have been described and analysed with the help of empirical evidences. Major problems related to development of tea industry and suggestions for policy implication are also the part of the discussion. Present work is based on author's doctoral level research work on the subject and serves as a useful reference material for those who wish to undertake the further, study on the different aspects of tea industry and trade.

Barua (1977a) made an attempt to prepare an input-output table and technological coefficient matrix for Assam. Though I-O coefficients matrix was already available for the country as a whole and some other states; but no concerted efforts were made to construct an I-O table for North Eastern Region as a whole or its constituent units. Though the current table is in an aggregate form, but it helps us to understand the intersectoral structure of the economy of state, Assam.

Barua (1977b) uses the I-O table of Assam in estimating the intersectoral linkages for the economy of Assam. It was found that commercial crop sector (raw Jute, Cotton, Sugar Cane and Oil Seeds etc.) has the largest single total linkages followed by the agrobased industries and mineral based manufacturing industries. This suggests that these sectors may be treated as key sectors and given priority, while preparing development strategy for the state.

Borthakur (1978) examined the status of the industrial sector in Assam and its growth since the beginning of the first five year plan. He studied the causes of industrial intertia and levels of growth of industrial employment. Author tried to relate the unemployment problem of the state with the very slow growth of industrialisation.

Passah (1980) analysed the trading practices adopted by indigenous people of Meghalaya in the context of prevailing socio-economic customary way of life. He revealed that some social disability emanating from the matrilineal system of inheritance does exist in society which particularly prevents the growth and uninterrupted development of trade and commerce among the tribes of Meghalaya. He suggested some positive changes in the existing social system which would encourage the trade and business potential of tribal people.

Sri Prakash (1984) in a study, tries to measure Capital coefficients in small scale industries and highlighted the inter firm, inter industry and intra-regional variations for the state Meghalaya. Study reveals that there had been a high degree of imbalance in industrial development within the state. He showed that fifty-one per cent of the total industrial firms of the state are located in the Khasi Hills alone. He also discussed the trend of industrial growth and associated problems and suggested measures towards improving the industrial environment in the state.

Upadhyaya (1986) studied the energy development prospects for the region. He projected the energy demand for the year 1990, and presented a case for hydro power generation to fulfil the growing demand for the region. He proposed to develop the railway net work in the region to improve the transport infra-structural facilities.

Barman (1987) analyses in detail the various aspects associated to the jute production in Assam, since 1951–78. He has estimated trend by computing compound growth rates of production and found negative growth rate for the period under study. The possible reasons for declining growth of jute production are also highlighted at length.

Mali and Deka (1987) published a book, which is a collection of sixteen selected papers presented at the seminar on "Small Industry Development", organised by the National Institute of Small Industry Extension and Training, North East Region Centre, Guwahati in August, 1985. It contains the papers contributed by eminent economists, planners, administrators and other social scientists of the region. The book presents a critical study of the different aspects of small industry development in the region. It discusses the various factors like, location, infrastructural facilities, finance, marketing and entrepreneurial issues etc. related to the existing small-scale industries in the region. It also, suggests numerous measures to encourage the faster and economically viable development of small scale industries in the region, such as, setting up a professionally managed regional level public sector organisation for solving the marketing problems, apex level organisation for co-ordinating the activities of promotional organisations, and entrepreneurship development. This book is useful for the students of industrial economics, planners, policy makers and administrators etc.

Sarmah (1987) attempts a review of small industry development in the region vis-a-vis in India. It is mentioned that the main bottlenecks in the industrial development in the region relates to transport, labour, marketing and entrepreneurship. It is also noticed, that in the large number of cases, the finance is not a problem but the problem is credit worthy proposal for bank finance. It is suggested that entrepreneurs are to be encouraged and trained to come forward for resource based industries.

Baruah (1987) makes an attempt to suggest a practical solution for developing the entrepreneurship talent in the region. The approach is based on an integrated model evolved and developed by National Institute of Small Industry Extension and Training, Guwahati. Author stressed that along with physical and economic infrastructure, there is a need to revamp social infrastructure in terms of community education, identification, selection training and institutional and social support to first generation entrepreneurs.

Bhat (1987) explores the possibility to look forward linkages of some small scale industries with large scale public sector in the region. According to author it is possible, by developing already identified small scale industries, to produce the ancillary units required by North-front railway sector. It was found that there is a vast scope for such industries to come forward and supply materials to railway sector.

Deka (1987) attempts to show how spatial aspects of small industry development can also play a decisive role in planning for development. Author expressed the opinion that any attempt of planning at district level must envisage a composite landscape of primary and secondary planning region. In this approach when nodes are ordered hierarchically, it is feasible to develop through higher order nodes to lower level centres. In this study author tries to relate the development of small scale industries with the growth centres of Kamrup district of Assam. Author identified the growth centres, their functions and infrastructural facilities and assessed their potentialities to support small industries in the district. The study may encourage the other researchers to undertake such type of studies for other districts of the north eastern region.

Goswami (1987) in his article advocated that development and expansion of secondary sector of the economy must be related to agricultural and allied activities. Accordingly it is necessary to evaluate the performance of existing small-scale industries in the light of potentiality of expansion of market for the goods produced by these units in the region. For solving the problem of marketing he proposed for a separate marketing organisation. Such an organisation may have different wings like marketing, technology development, training, finance and credit, etc. The major role of this apex body will be to co-ordinate the activities in the desired direction, monitor and evaluate progress and suggest measures for development.

Neog (1988) has made an attempt to evaluate the strategies problems and potentialities of industrialisation for balanced regional development of the region. The development gap of the nation as a whole, vis-a-vis the developed world and of north east India, vis-a-vis all India level are estimated and the development scenario for the year 2000 AD is projected. Comparing Indian economy, in per capita income terms, the economy of Assam is lagging behind by over 43 years with respect to all India average.

Sectoral inter dependence of the national and regional economy is estimated by using econometric techniques. Author suggests a resource base industrialisation of the region in order to accelerate the industrial development and economic growth of the region.

Deb (1988) analyses the status of economic development of NER and the role of infra-structural sector with the help of district statistics collected from secondary sources. It was found that the development of infrastructural sector is inadequate both qualitatively and quantitatively in the region. The author proposed for massive organisational efforts for mobilising both human and natural resources in a well synchronised manner.

Bhuyan (1988) stresses on the important role of institutional and other economic infrastructural facilities in developing an industrial climate and economic environment in the region. On the basis of interstate comparisons it was evolved that north eastern region suffers from various gaps, like communication, implementation and co-ordination of planning efforts. Unless these gaps are bridged by developing requisite infrastructural facilities, the industrial and economic environment conducive to development would not improve in this region.

An account of infrastructural development in the economy of Meghalaya during five year plans, is available with Passah (1988). The growth rate and changes in the pattern of investment analysed in order to notice the progress in power generation, transport, education and health and services sector. It was concluded that in spite of the moderate development of this factor during five year plans, it is still weak to sustain any rigorous program of industrialisation and improvement of agricultural sector in the state.

Electronic industries are considered environmental friendly industries and also require energy consumption with less used material inputs. Nevertheless, utility potentials of electronic devices are immense and if economies of scale are properly exploited the production of such commodities can take place in a cost effective manner. Hazarika (1988) explores the scope for the development of electronic industry in the region. For this purpose author has analysed in detail the nature of electronic industry, along with flow charts explaining structure and stages of production of this industry. Author supports the idea of establishing electronic industry with the help of direct support of state governments to initiate the process.

Saikia (1988) analyses in detail the scope of resource based industries in NER. Some of such industries are identified like agro-chemical industries for pesticides and fertilisers. Other resource based industries like cement plants, petrochemicals and paper and pulp industries are also important for the region. These industries do have very high backward linkages and can play very important role in industrialising the region.

State has taken a number of direct and indirect measures to promote industrial sector during five year plans. One of the institutional measures initiated by the Government of India was the Industrial Estate Program, initiated at the beginning of second five year plan. Mali and Baruah (1988) discuss the major objectives of this program and its status and growth in NER. Total employment generation and products manufactured by the industries under this scheme are highlighted. Authors conclude that the Industrial Estate Program has helped a lot in creating an industrial climate and has encouraged the prospective entrepreneurs to take up industrial activities in small scale industrial sector.

Resource based industrialisation generates an additional demand of inputs derived from natural resources. North eastern part of India is well known for its rich variety of natural resources derived from forests. Moreover, this region has a sizable population of tribals, living in and around forests on which they depend heavily for their subsistence. They practice Jhum cultivation, collect fuel fodder, fruit and other forest products. Forestry operations provide them employment as well. Agarwal (1988) analyses forestry development and suggests an approach to deal with forestry development problems. Author proposes involvement of a suitable village organisation for promoting plantation activities in the village, common lands and for private land on mutually beneficial terms, with proper safeguard for rights and privileges of the dwellers, as well as the administration. The proper forestry development programs should include the protection of forests in the hills, control of shifting cultivation and permanent settlement of Jhumia families.

Technology plays an important role in modernising the production process and economic advancement of the economy. Sengupta (1989) made an attempt to analyse the technological development in farm sector. This study is based on statistic collected from national sample survey on the estimated number of the agricultural machines and different non farm business equipments owned per hundred household by size class of household operational holdings in the state Meghalaya. Statistics reveal very low or negligible use of modern equipment in farming. It is concluded that the major reasons for this dismal picture may be, poverty of the people, a lack of interest to innovate and a sense of satisfaction with the prevailing situation. Study lacks in-depth analysis of the relationship between size class of households and use of the types of machinery and equipments.

Baisya (1989) presents a micro level study of small and cottage industries in Assam based on field investigations. It also, traces the industrial development process in Assam in a historical perspective. Study highlights the various aspects of small scale industries like inputs, employment procurement of raw materials, working expenses, marketing, productivity, wages and potentialities in detail. The author has, also, analysed the problems faced by the industries in modernisation of production process, plants and machineries, designs, competition from other areas and sectors, higher costs and inefficiencies of production. It was observed in the analysis that while the traditional village industries have been declining, the performance of the modern small-scale industries have shown encouraging upward trend. As it is also admitted by the author, this study is more of diagnostic nature rather than based on statistical estimation projections, which becomes a major limitation of the study.

Upadhyaya (1989) made an attempt to develop a tentative input-output table for Mizoram for the year 1987–88 at local prices for the same year. An aggregated sectoral level I-O table covers more than 80 per cent of total state domestic products, for the state Mizoram. The agriculture, energy and construction sectors were emerged as major economic sectors in the economy of Mizoram. This study needs a systematic in-depth analysis of the inter-sectoral dependence and linkage analysis of the state economy.

Mali (1989) made an attempt to study the development of tribal entrepreneurship in North Eastern region by tracing the social origin of entrepreneurship. The study reveals that distribution of entrepreneurs is not proportional to the size of social groups. Tribal entrepreneurs are present only in those region, where entry of non-tribal entrepreneurs is difficult for one reason or the other. In other regions the distribution of tribal entrepreneurs is proportionately low. The observations made by the study have deep implications related to entrepreneurship development in the region.

Development of infrastructural facilities has a strong relationship with the enhancement of standard of living, broadens the socio-economic awareness of the people and brings the modernity in all walks of life. Kallurao and Pai (1990) analyses the development of this sector in the state, Manipur. The statistics for this study has been collected from the publications of the Directorate of Economics and Statistics, Government of Manipur. To find out the concentration of household on their operational holdings, the estimation of

Index of inter-class concentration, location quotient, and balancing ratios are applied for the purpose of analysis. It was found that the availability of infrastructural facilities are inadequate and inequitably distributed. Deficit areas have been identified and study proposed for greater attention on the development of such areas of state on priority basis.

Dutta (1990) evaluates the performance of public sector in Tripura. Author has prepared and analysed a profitability profile for the period 1981–82 to 1984–85 based on annual reports, financial records, account books of the public sector undertakings of the state. Author suggests the measures for improving overall operational efficiency of existing public sectors. It is concluded that revitalisation of these public sectors require a dynamic management capable of taking and pragmatic decisions on appropriate time.

Prasad (1990) discusses in depth, the approach to the industrial development of the north eastern region and highlighted the factors inhibiting industrialisation. Author stressed on the need of an industrial policy which is based on the linkages with agricultural development. It is proposed that the priority may be given to forest, livestock and mineral based industries. In view of the very limited managerial, technical and skilled manpower for large-scale projects, it would be more appropriate to give preference to small-scale units having improved technology.

Goenka (1990) made an attempt to evaluate the strategy for industrial development of the region. Author analyses the existing status of industrialisation along with major constraints to industrial growth. Incidence of high transportation and capital costs and the degree of its adverse impact on industrial output production is mentioned as the major obstacle to faster industrial growth.

It is noteworthy that Bardhan (1990) under took a study on the small scale industries of Tripura, one of industrially least advanced states of North Eastern India. In the absence of large-scale industries, the small scale industries including the cottage and village industries have been playing significant contribution to the State Domestic Product (SDP) of the state. Author pointed out the there is a scope for further expansion of the small-scale industries in order to absorb the growing unemployment in the state.

References

Agarwal, A.K. (1988), "Forestry Development in the North-East: An Approach", in Ram Prakash (ed.), *Advance of Forestry Research in India*, Vol. II, International Book Distributors, Deheradun 105–116.

Agarwal, A.K. (1989), "Planning in Arunachal Pradesh : Overall View and Policy Implication" in Bhattacharjee, J.B., *Sequence of Development in North East India*, Omsons Publications, Delhi, 103–117.

Awasthi, R.C. (1975), *Economics of Tea Industry in India with special reference to Assam*, United Publishers, Guwahati.

Baishya, P.(1989), *Small and Cottage Industries: A Study in Assam*, Manas Publications, Delhi.

Bardhan, G. (1990), "Problems and Prospects of Small Scale Industries in Tripura" in R.K. Rai et al. (eds.), *Hill Area Development*, The Geographical Society of North-Eastern Region, Shillong.

Barman, K.K. (1987), "Growth of Jute Production in Assam: 1951–78, Is it Decelerating?, *North East Quarterly*, April–June, Vol. 2, 1–15.

Barthakur, M. (1978), "Industrial Inertia and Growth of Industrial Employment in Assam Since 1951", *North Eastern Geographer*, Vol. 10, No. 1 & 2, 1–6.

Baruah, A.R. (1987), "Developing Entrepreneurship in North East Region: An Approach", in Mali, D.D. and Deka, P. (eds.), Omsons Publications, New Delhi, 95–109.

Baruah, S. (1977a), "Input-Output Coefficient Matrix for Assam: An Approximation (1969)", *North Eastern Economic Review*, Vol. I, No. 1.

Baruah, S. (1977b), "The Identification of Key Sectors in the Economy of Assam", *North Eastern Economic Review*, Vol. I, No. 3.

Bhat, M.S. (1987), "Small Industries and Railway Purchases", in Mali, D.D. and Deka, P. (eds.), Omsons Publications, New Delhi, 145–152.

Bhuyan, J. (1988), "Economic Infrastructure in North-Eastern State" in D. Bhorali (ed.), Spectrum Publications, Guwahati, 40–45.

Deb (1988), "Development of NER: What Role Infrastructure Plays", in D. Bhorali (ed.) *Economic Development of North-Eastern Region*, Spectrum Publications, Guwahati, 21–32.

Deka, C. (1987), "Growth Centres in Small Industry Development: A Case Study of Kamrup District ", in Mali, D.D. and Deka, P. (eds.), Omsons Publications, New Delhi, 153–166.

Dutta, N.C. (1990), "Public Sector Undertakings in Tripura—A Study of their Performance", *Journal of North-East India Council for Social Science Research*, April 14,1, 54–61.

Goenka, P.C. (1990), "Strategy for Industrial Development of North-East Region", in Barua P.C. (ed.), Mittal Publications, New Delhi, 195–223.

Goswami (1987), "A Note on Development of Small-Scale Industries in North East India", in Mali, D.D. and Deka, P. (eds.), Omsons Publications, New Delhi, 1–8.

Hazarika, S. (1988), "Scope for Electronics Industry in North-Eastern Region", in D. Bhorali (ed.), Spectrum Publications, Guwahati, 145–154.

Kallurao, P., and Pai, V.S. (1990), "Infrastructural Facilities in Manipur: A Study", *Journal of North-East India Council for Social Science Research*, April, 14,1, 22–32.

Mali, D.D. (1989), "Development of Tribal Entrepreneurship in North-East Region: Problems & Prospects", *Journal of the North-Eastern Council*, Shillong, XI, 5, January–March, 2–4.

Mali, D.D. and Baruah, A.R. (1988), "Growth of Industrial Estates in the NER", in D. Bhorali (ed.), Spectrum Publications, Guwahati, 167–176.

Mali, D.D. and Deka, P. (1987) (eds.), *Industrial Development in North East India*, Omsons Publications, New Delhi.

Neog, A.K. (1988), "Role of Industry in the Economic Development of North East India: Projections for 2000 AD", in Thakur, P. (ed.), *Profile of a Development Strategy for India's North East*, Span Publications Pvt. Ltd., Guwahati, 139–164.

Passah, P.M. (1980), "Trading by Meghalayans—The Impact of their Matrilineal System of Inheritance there on", in Mathew, T. (ed.), *Tribal Economy of the North East Region*, Spectrum Publications, Guwahati, 144–153.

Passah, P.M. (1988), "Infrastructure Development in Meghalaya", in D. Bhorali (ed.), Spectrum Publications, Guwahati, 67–75.

Prasad, Kamta. (1990), "An Approach to the Industrial Development of the North-Eastern Region", in Barua, P.C. (ed.), *Development Planning of North-East India*, Mittal Publications, New Delhi, 133–148.

Sakia, C.N. (1988), "Scope of Industrial Development of NER", in D. Bhorali (ed.), Spectrum Publications, Guwahati,155–166.

Sarmah, H.C.(1987), "Industrial Development in North East India: A Review of Development of Small-Scale Sector", in Mali, D.D. and Deka, P. (eds.), Omsons Publications, New Delhi, 75–94.

Sengupta, Keya (1989), "The Use of Technology in North-Eastern States: A Case Study of Meghalaya", *Journal of North-East India Council for Social Science Research*, October, 13,2, 17–23.

Sri Prakash, (1984), "Capital Coefficients in Small-Scale Industries in Meghalaya: A Study of Inter-Firm, Inter-Industry and Intra-Regional Variations", *Hill geographer*, Vol. 3, No. 1, 1–15.

Upadhyaya, K.K. (1986), "Energy Development Prospects for North Eastern India", *Urja*, Vol. 19, No. 4, 259–263.

Upadhyaya, K.K. (1989), "Input-Output Table for Mizoram: 1987–88", *Indian Journal of Regional Science*, 21,2, 72–75.

VIII

DEMOGRAPHY

The population of North-Eastern of Region of India accounts for 31.5 million, which is 3.7 per cent of the country's total population as per the population census 1991. Though population density is low in this region, but in respect of population composition and associated demographic and socio-economic characteristics the region is quite distinct from rest of the country. The region has long history of human migrations from north and south east Asia, belonging to various races, ethno-linguistic groups and cultures. It is interesting to note that inspite of regions geographical isolation and difficult terrain condition, people belonging to different ethnic groups have entered in to it from different directions at different point of times.

There are about 450 tribes in India, out of which about 150 tribes are in north east India. The tribal population of the region constitutes 26 per cent of the regions total population which accounts for 12 per cent of the country's total tribal population. The north-east region of India is also known as 'the land of tribes'. Besides tribals, people from all the linguistic and religious groups of the country are also residing in this part of country. All these varieties have provided fertile fields for under taking demographic studies on the various facets of economic analysis. Economic development and population dynamics are so closely interlinked that it is necessary to take into account the demographic dimensions for understanding the aspects of social and economic development of any region.

This creates the need for proper demographic studies in order to capture the demographic scenario and imbedded changes taken place time to time in north east part of India. The worth mentioning efforts in this direction are Das (1980),

Guha (1980) and Roy Barman (1980) who have analysed in detail the demographic transformation of Assam since the beginning of twentieth century till the year 1970–71. It was concluded that, the migration has not been a contributing factor to Assam's alarming growth of population and Assam's abnormally high rate of growth of population is basically an outcome of its own higher rate of natural increase resulting from very high birth rate and lowered death rate.

Ganguli (1983) analyses the population trends in Tripura during last one hundred years. Author discusses the distribution of tribal population and its occupation, along with agrarian structure, literacy, decadal variation, population density and sex-ratio etc. are discussed from 1931–1981. Analysing the empirical evidences derived from the variations in the composition of economic classification of population, author concludes that pre 1951 immigration didn't lead to the improvement in the prospect of sustained economic growth although it brought about some administration, education and transport development. However, book lacks adequate analysis of the demographic factors and their impact on socio-economic aspects of the area under study.

In an empirical study based on the time series data on the population of Assam for seventy years from the year 1900–1971, Goswami (1984) observed that population increase in Assam during this period has been of 315 per cent, while it was only 135 per cent for the country as a whole for the same period. Author claims that this high growth in population is indicative of high level of immigration and migration to the region. This has changed the demographic structure of the region on the one hand, and creates pressure on economic resources on the other hand. Author suggests a practical and constructive approach must be made to solve this crisis amicably within the given time framework. Social and Economic change in Manipur edited by Ahluwalia and Ahluwalia (1984) is a collection of articles by various scholars on Manipuri language, literature and demography. Authors have presented the account of the origin, migration and the organisation of villages. Some authors have also tried to study the impact of the outside world on the traditional life-style of the tribes of Manipur.

Goswami and Gogoi (1984) express the need to view the problem of migration and demographic transformation of Assam from historical point of view. They observed that the rate of flow of population was substantially high during 1941–71, the rising rate was highest during 1951–61. Author expressed the view of adverse impact of this inflow on socio-economic development of the region.

Saikia (1984) analysed the decennial growth rate of population of Assam and compared it with other states of India. It also completes the relationship between population density with average size of land holding, net sown area per cultivator. It was observed that continuous influx of immigrants is mainly responsible for the rate of growth of population, which has created a complex economic situation. Indigenous people found it difficult to compete with immigrants especially in trade and commerce as these have skill and strong financial support base. Immigrant agricultural labourers have made the indigenous worker poorer because agriculture is their only source of lively hood. Author also draws attention to the differential problems of the plains and hill people.

Dattaray (1986) edited a volume on the pattern and problems of population in north east India. This book is the outcome of the seminar organised by north-east India council for social science research, Shillong, in December, 1984. Besides economists, demographers, statisticians, geographers, anthropologists and other social scientists have also contributed their research papers. Studies touches the areas of physical features like distribution and density pattern, migration, employment and unemployment structure along with quality features like health and nutrition status, literacy rates, social participation, human resource development, production and social justice etc. This work will be useful for the students and research scholars tend to pursue the work in the fields of demographic and related areas.

Sharma (1986) analyses the socio-economic characteristics of north-eastern India. The issues related to fertility and family planning are highlighted with the help of theoretical frame work and empirical evidences. Author has explained the observed decline in morality and fertility of the region due to spread of education and improvement in health facilities rather than the changes in macro economic conditions.

In a study on the migrants in north-eastern region Sebastian (1986) explained the aspects related to various types of inter state/inter regional migrations on the basis of migration differentials with respect to age and sex. In a comparative study of life time internal and external migrants based on place of birth and place of last residence shows that place of birth data gives a better estimates of migrants to this region.

Worth mentioning attempt has been made to explain the relatively higher growth of population of Assam since independence in Alam (1986). With the help of empirical evidences author correlates the high rate of growth of population with low proportion of area under cultivation, low man land ratio, small size of land holding, inequality in the ownership of land, landlessness and diminishing agricultural output, income per worker and dwindling food availability. It is concluded that heavy population on land in Assam is the generation of considerable magnitude of disguised unemployment in rural areas.

Choudhary (1986) studied systematically the changes in age patterns of Assam's population during 1961–71 and it's impact on economic activities. For this purpose the dependency ratio is estimated along with variations in age structure at district level. It is found that there has been an overall increase in the percentage of children in the decade. The dependency burden on adult has increased during the decade in the state.

Bose, Nongbri and Nikhlesh Kumar (1990) present a volume of edited articles. This book is the outcome of research papers presented to symposium on tribal demography in collaboration with Jawahar Lal Nehru University's, Imphal Centre in Manipur in 1976. Research papers are arranged in three subsections, namely, perspective and issues in development, population patterns, occupational structure and nutrition, health and education. There are twenty research articles written by economists, sociologists and other social scientists included in the volume.

References

Ahluwalia, B.K. and Shashi Ahluwalia (1984) (eds.), *Social Change in Manipur*, Cultural Publishing House, New Delhi.

Alam, K. (1986), "Population explosion and it's impact on the Economy of Assam", in Dattaray, B., (ed.), Uppal Publishing House, New Delhi, 191–200.

Bose, Ashish, Tilput Nongbri and Nikhlesh Kumar (1990) (eds.), *Tribal Demography and Development in North-East India*, D.K. Publishers, New Delhi.

Choudhary, D.C. (1986), "Change of Age Pattern of Assam's Population During 1961 and 1971 and it's Impact on Economic Activities", in Dattaray, B. (ed.), Uppal Publishing House, New Delhi, 209–226.

Das S.K. (1980), "Immigration and demographic Transformation of Assam, 1891–1981", *Economic and Political Weekly*, May 10, 52–73.

Dattaray, B. (1986) (ed.), *The Pattern and Problems of Population in North-East India*, Uppal Publishing House, New Delhi.

Ganguli, J.B. (1983), *The Benigh Hills: A Study in Tripura's Population Growth & Problems*, Tripura Darpan Prakashan, Agartala.

Goswami, A. and Gogoi J.K. (1984), *Migration and Demographic Transformation of Assam: 1901–1971*, in Abbi, B.L. (ed.), Centre for Research in Rural and Industrial Development, Chandigarh, 60–80.

Goswami, P.C. (1984), "Foreign Immigration in to Assam", in Abbi B.L. (ed.), *North-east Region Problems and Prospects of Development*, Centre for Research in Rural and Industrial Development, Chandigarh, 35–59.

Guha, A. (1980) "Little Nationalism Turned Chauvinist : Assam's Anti-Foreigner Upsurge: 1979–80", *Economic & Political Weekly*, Special Number, 19–27.

Roy Burman, B.K. (1980), "North-East India : An Overview", *Mainstream*, December, 6, 8–10.

Saikia P.D. (1984), "Present and future of North-East India : Land and Population Explosion", in Abbi, B.L. (ed.), *North-Eastern Region: Problems and Prospects of Development*, Centre for Research in Rural and Industrial Development, Chandigarh, April, 81–94.

Sebastian, A. (1986), "Migrants in North-Eastern Region of India", in Dattaray, B. (ed.), Uppal Publishing House, New Delhi, 63–88.

Sharma, A.K. (1986), "Population of North-Eastern Zone of India: Patterns and Problems", in Dattaray B. (ed.), Uppal Publishing House, New Delhi, 51–61.

IX

HUMAN RESOURCE DEVELOPMENT

Economic resources are generally of two types, namely human and non-human resources. The human resource includes the knowledge, the skills and the capacities of the people of a region to undertake the process of production. Development of human resources not only uplifts productivity in economic sectors but also creates further favourable atmosphere for investment in the economy. Economists now concede that the main cause of economic backwardness has been the underdevelopment of human resource. Therefore, such economies need investment on education, research training, know-how and higher level of physical efficiency of people for faster economic development. Some studies under review address the issues of human resources. Whereas, other studies emphasises on status of manpower planning, its relevance and prospects in north eastern region.

Discussing the detailed account of the status, problems and prospects of human resource development and man power planning in the north-eastern region, Sing (1982) has made an attempt based on statistical evidences. This study is based on secondary data collected from various sources and presented in the form of highly suggestive and systematic manner. Author has taken five states and two union territories (as were prevailing during the period of study) as the units of his study. Study analysed the ethnic, linguistic and regional heterogeneity of the region. It also analyses and compared the interaction between the level of human resources and the level of amenities available to them. The book is very useful to the researchers of economics discipline, who want to study the human resource status and its relationship with perspective development of the region.

Shukla and Agarwal (1983) present a research paper based on statistic of cultivators and agricultural labourers from the census of India 1981. Analysing the percentage distribution of main workers by cultivators, agricultural labourers and other workers in north-east region 1961–81. It is observed that absolute number of agricultural labourers has increased at a faster rate in all the states of the region, which has caused a small size of holdings. Also, the percentage of female work force has increased with a faster rate then the male work force. Further, the problems of agricultural labourers are not so intense in states where land is community owned but disguised unemployment is certainly there. Authors suggest the implementation of state sponsored developmental programs and the participation of villagers would definitely help in solving the problems of migration of agricultural labourers from rural to urban areas in search of employment.

Bhattacharya (1984) stressed the relevance of manpower planning for the faster industrialisation of the so far backward economy of the state Tripura. Author mainly studied three aspects, namely, demand for skilled manpower dictated by the industriliasation, supply of skilled manpower at present and potential and policy measures for optimum interaction between demand and supply to promote economic growth and social welfare. Assessing the situation author expressed the opinion that skill formation for industrial development in Tripura has to be achieved more through expanding non formal job oriented technical education.

Lawma (1986) in his paper examines the degree and nature of relationship between occupation and earning and between earning and pattern of high level of education in north-east India on the basis of vacancies advertised both in private and public organisations over a period of one year. Author concludes, that the earning differentials are significantly dependent upon the period of experiences in the services or on training rather than on education alone. The paper concludes that educated unemployment is mainly due to the sluggish economy and therefore, enhanced production is suggested for opening up the doors of employment opportunities to them.

Lawma and Sri Prakash (1986) tried to estimate the desired levels and patterns of educational qualifications of manpower industry and occupation-wise in the north-east India. It was concluded that for most of the occupations, levels and patterns of required qualification vary making salaries and grades also vary across the industries. Furthermore, higher emoluments are carried by those fields of education specialisation occupation for which supplies are relatively low.

Lawma (1990) made an attempt to explain the functioning of labour markets in general and the markets for the educational manpower particularly in north-eastern region. With the help of levels and types of education, occupation and various sectors of the economy, the patterns between inter and intra regional migrants are also established. Manpower markets imperfections are highlighted on the basis of actual practice of hiring and placement of labour and the availability of skill in market. This study is an example of systematic and scientific use of research techniques in understanding the factor market imperfections and manpower planning in North-Eastern region. The book is useful for planners, policy makers and students of manpower planning and labour economics.

Goel and Mishra (1990) studied the spatial pattern of literacy and its disparities among various communities in Senapati District of Manipur. Study reveals a spatial pattern of literacy in the region. Paper deals the status of education in tribal area and found that literacy differ from tribe to tribe in the region.

References

Bhattacharya, P.R. (1984), "Manpower Planning and Industrialisation of Tripura" *Journal of North-East India Council for Social Science Research*, Shillong, October, Vol. 8, No. 2, 1–5.

Goel, N.P. and Mishra, S.K. (1990), "Disparities in Educational Achievement of Various Communities in Manipur: A Study of Senapati District", in Rai, R.K. et al. (eds.), *Hill Area Development: Issues and Perspectives*, Geographical Society of the North Eastern Hill Region, Shillong, 166–172.

Lawma, T. (1986), "Earning-Occupation-Education; Inter-Relations: A Case Study of North East India", *The Manpower Journal*, Institute of Applied Manpower Research, Vol. XXII, No. 1, 1–28.

Lawma, T. (1990), *Market Imperfections and Manpower Planning*, Commonwealth Publishers, New Delhi.

Lawma, T. and Sri Prakash (1986). "Levels and Patterns of Educational Qualifications of Manpower in North Eastern Region of India: A Study of Inter Industry and Occupational Variations of Demand", *NEHU Journal if Social Science and Humanities*, Shillong, IV, I, 29–44.

Shukla, S.P. and A.K. Agrawal (1983), "The Magnitude of the Problem of Agricultural Labour in the North-East Region", *Journal of North-East India Council for Social Science Research*, April, Vol. 7, No. 1, 34–38.

Sing, J.P. (1982), *Human Resources of North-East India*, Inter-India Publications. New Delhi.

X

GENERAL

This section discusses the miscellaneous studies, which couldn't classify within the framework of previously discussed sections. These research efforts are important because these are based on more specific and specialised fields of economics. Some of these studies belong to emerging fields of economics, therefore, don't come under the preview of traditional economics, whereas some other studies address the contemporary and relatively modern economic issues of the north eastern region. One of such branch of economics is transport economics. Transport is a vital infrastructural sector for economic development and well being. Surface transport in the form of railways and road are both needed for resource mobilisation within the region and outside the region.

Medhi (1978) undertakes a methodological study of the transport system in Assam, beginning with a study in back ground, through an analysis, the various modes of transport, their inter relationship and impact on the economic development of North-East region. This book is a notable contribution to understand the problems of an isolated region (such as Assam) in obtaining adequate transport facilities and the problems of the transport operators in providing them.

The book is divided in four parts. The first part is primarily concerned with historical back-ground. Part II is an analysis of the impact of railways on various sectors of the economy. In part III, a study of railway freight rates and its coordination to appraise the impact of railways as compared to other modes of transport. In part IV, a scheme for increasing railway facilities, which might enable the railways to exert better impact on the economy, has been outlined.

In an techno-economic study, Bora (1988) projected the passenger trip production and forecasts for the year 1993–94. Inland water and air transport within the region is also explored. The employment potential of various mode of transportation are estimated and compared for energy efficient planning. For an appropriate transport planning author emphasises that strong data base would facilitate the realistic transport demand projection, transport option computability, which can be treated as base for viable developmental strategy for the region.

Goswami, (1979) presents a book based on his Ph.D. thesis entitled "Prices and cost of living in Assam: 1951–1970". It is a study of the behaviour of prices and cost of living in the wider setting of the national economy. An attempt has been made in study to brought together the scattered price and cost of living statistics for Assam in a comprehensive and scientific manner. The study examines the trend, seasonal variations and random fluctuations of prices along with cost of living of various population groups in Assam. Author also identifies the factors influencing the price movements in Assam.

Analysing the time series data on price fluctuation it is observed that prices are in general higher in NE region as compared to the rest of country. The unusually high rate of growth of population, stagnancy of agriculture, decline in marketable surplus, hoarding, monopoly element in distribution are mainly responsible for upward price movements. Author suggests the strengthening public distribution systems could be a short term solution to deal with prevailing situation. The book is useful for the researchers in the field of economics and related subjects.

Barua (1989) surveyed the development of the banking industry with particular reference to north-east India. It is pointed out that considerable expansion of the banking as well as other financial institution had been made in recent years in India but this region is lagged behind. A full scale investigation of the demand and supply of banking services is needed to find out the causes of low off-take of credit, indifferent attitude of public and low productivity and efficiency in banking sector. Author suggests that it would be helpful in strengthening the cooperatives and appointing individuals as agents for deposit mobilisation in remote areas.

Goswami and Kalita (1990) are of the view that for rapid economic development the expansion of banking sector is very much required which plays an important role in capital formation, credit creation and to fulfil the aspirations of entrepreneur's financial requirements. They have analysed the bank-wise performance of branch expansion and state wise distribution of centres with banking facilities. It was noticed that from the year 1981 to 1987 the maximum number of bank branches are opened in Assam followed by Tripura, Meghalaya, Mizoram, Arunachal Pradesh and Nagaland.

Recent developments in public finance in the fields of fiscal theory and policy have been, by and large, on regional lines. But in the north-eastern states very few studies are available in published form, which analyses systematically the regional fiscal economics. One such attempt is made by Bhuyan (1983) to study the regional fiscal economics of Assam. This study is based on state budget of twenty eight years from 1951–52 to 1978–79, analyses in detail the growth of revenues and state expenditures, their trends and changes in the pattern, shared taxes and grants-in-aids in the light of various finance commision reports. The book is divided in four parts (14 chapters in all) devoted to tax and non-tax revenues, public expenditures capital formation and public debts for the state Assam.

Although this book can't serve as a comprehensive text book on public finance yet it is of immense use for the students and scholars interested in empirical analysis of state budgeting and under standing the behavioural dynamics of regional fiscal economics at state level in general and Assam in particular.

In another worth mentioning attempt Dass (1987) studied the fiscal structure of Assam for the period 1964–65 to 1978–79. This work is the extension of Ph.D. thesis submitted by the author to Jawaharlal Nehru University, New Delhi. Author analyses the reponsiveness of productivity of state taxes in Assam by estimating the vertical and horizontal equity of tax burden. The state taxes are divided in four groups: all Assam taxes, Inter-expenditure class equity estimates and intra-sectoral equity of state taxes, state direct taxes, total direct taxes and all state indirect taxes for the purpose of analysis. Important findings are dervied on the basis of inter-sectoral equity of state taxes. This work is useful for researchers interested in public finance and fiscal policy.

References

Barua, M.P. (1989), " Banking Industry and Rural Development in North-East India", in Sakai P.D. and Phukan, U. (eds.), *Rural Development in North-East India*, D.K. Publishing Distribution (p) Ltd, Delhi, 97–110.

Bhuyan, P.K. (1984), *The Regional Fiscal Economics of Assam*, Chugh Publications, Allahabad.

Bora, P. (1988), "Strategy for the Development of Transport facilities in NER with sights set in 21st Century", in Pankaj Thakur (ed.), *Profile of a Development Strategy for India's North East*, Span Publications Pvt. Ltd., Guwahati, 77–110.

Dass, S.K. (1987), *Dynamics of Taxation in a Developing Economy with Special Reference to Assam*, 1964–65 to 1978–79, Omsons Publications, New Delhi.

Goswami, A. (1979), *Prices and Cost of Living in India*, Jain Book Depot, New Delhi.

Goswami, S.N. and Kalita, D.R. (1990), "Regional Imbalances in Banking Development—The Case of NE Region", *Journal of North-East India Council for Social Science and Research*, April, Vol. 14, No. 1, 33–77.

Medhi, S.B. (1978), *Transport System and Economic Development in Assam*, Publication Board, Assam, Gauhati.

APPRAISAL OF PH.D. LEVEL RESEARCH ON THE NORTH EASTERN REGION

Doctoral dissertation constitutes a very pertinent component of research work in any subject branch of knowledge and region. A good number of Ph.D. degrees are also awarded in Economics in the universities of the North Eastern Region. An attempt is made to appraise the research in the field of Economics during the period 1970–90 in the region. This analysis is based on the statistics available in the various bibliographies published by the Documentation and Data Analysis Unit of NEHU Library and ICSSR (NERC), Shillong. The M.Phil dissertations could not be included in this analysis as full information was not available.

As Gauhati University is the oldest university in the region, it has contributed the highest number of Ph.D. degrees in Economics. The total production of Ph.D. dissertations by all other universities together in the region is much less than the number the Gauhati University has alone produced, as other universities established much later.

Table 1 presents a By-way classification of Ph.D. thesis awarded in Economics in the universities of North East India during the period 1970–1990. This classification is both year and theme-wise. Analysing the table, it is found that highest number of thesis (19.8%) are awarded in the field of Development Economics, followed by Agricultural Economics (17.3%). Industrial Economics and Demography share the equal numbers of Ph.D. thesis, i.e., (10.7%) each of the total Ph.Ds. awarded during the period. Relatively, less number of Ph.Ds. awarded in the field of Transport Economics, Economic Planning, Human Resource Development, Land Economics and

Table 1: By-way classification of Ph.D. thesis awarded in Economics in the universities of North-Eastern India (1970–1990)

Code No.	Theme	1970	71	72	73	74	75	76	77	78	79	80	81	82	83	84	85	86	87	88	89	90	Total
1	Agricultural Economics			1			2	1		1		3			2	1	2	3	1	1	1	2	21 (17.3)
2	Rural Economics					1				1			1				1		2		1	2	9 (7.4)
3	Land Economics												1				2				2		5 (4.1)
4	Industrial Economics	1		1									1	1		1	1	1	1		2	3	13 (10.7)
5	Economic System				1			1					1	1		1							5 (4.1)
6	Economic Planning							1	1										1				3 (2.5)
7	Economic Development	1		1		1	1	2		1	2	1	1	3	1	2			3		4		24 (19.8)
8	Demography		1					1	1	3			1	1	1		1			2	1		13 (10.7)
9	Human Resource Development						1											1	1				3 (2.5)
10	Public Finance			1			1	1	1				1						2			1	8 (6.6)
11	Transport Economics											1				1							2 (1.7)
12	Miscellaneous*				1		1				1	1	1		1	3			3			3	15 (12.4)
	Total	2	1	4	2	2	6	7	3	6	3	6	8	6	5	9	7	5	14	3	11	11	121 (100)

* Miscellaneous includes—Banking, Urbanisation, Foreign Aid, Trade, Price Movements, Consumer Behaviour & Labour Economics.

Note: Figures sin parentheses show the percentage.

Source: Documentation Unit of NEHU Library and ICSSR (NERC), Shillong.

Economic System. Least number of Ph.Ds. awarded in the fields of Banking, Urbanisation, Foreign Aid, Trade, Price Movement, Consumer Behaviour and Labour Economics, so are clubbed together in miscellaneous category in Table 1. The theme-wise Ph.Ds. awarded in Economics during the period are demonstrated in Fig. 1.

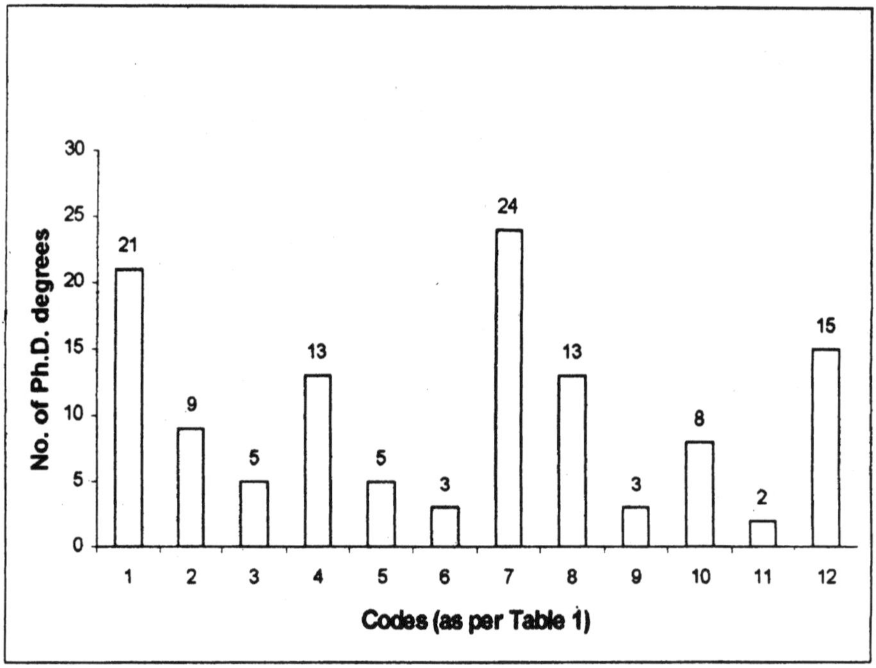

Fig. 1. Themes of Ph.D. degrees awarded in Economics (1970–90)

Table 2 presents the temporal distribution of Ph.D. dissertations awarded during the period of study. This table is derived from table 1.

Table 2: Temporal distribution of Ph.D. dissertations in NE Region

Year	Ph.D. dissertations	
	in Numbers	in Percentage
1970–1974	11	9.1
1975–1979	25	20.7
1980–1984	34	28.1
185–1990	51	42.1
Total	121	100

Source: Table 1.

The Ph.D. dissertations in Economics are also arranged in the form of temporal frequency distribution (Table 2) and demostrated in histogram (Fig. 2) in five years class interval. Analysing this time series, it is found that while only 9.1 percent Ph.D.'s awarded during the period 1970–1974, in onward periods this percentage is continuously increasing and reaching the peak during the period 1985–1990, where 42.1 percent of Ph.D. degrees were awarded. As an average six Ph.D. degrees per year in Economics are being awarded in the region during the period.

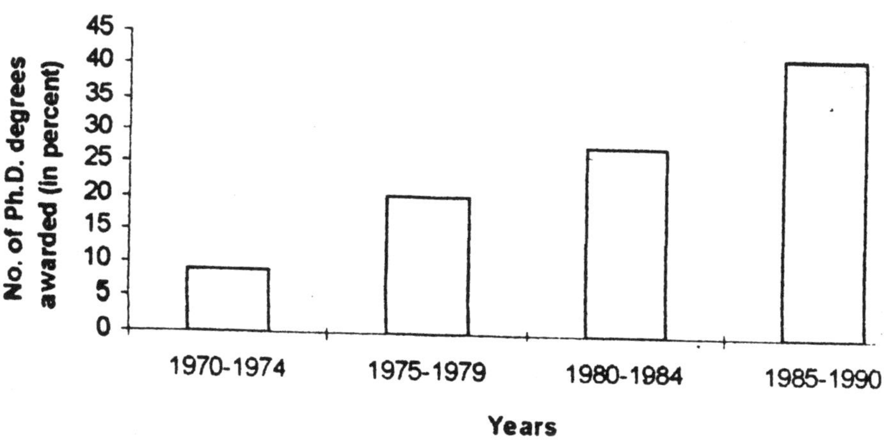

Fig. 2. Temporal Distribution of Ph.D. Dissertation in Economics

This accelerating growth in doctoral level reseach is a very encouraging trend, which implies that recently more and more young social scientists are paying attention towards the contemporary economic issues of the region. Emergence of new universities, departments and research institutions may certainly be a significant factor in explaining the temporal growth of Ph.D. awardees. It is hoped that this healthy trend will continue in future and would contribute significantly in the growth of Economics as a lively discipline of social sciences in the region.

BIBLIOGRAPHY

Ph.D. Dissertations

Ahmed, Atikuddin: The Anatomy of Rural Poverty in Dibrugarh District of Assam, Dibrugarh University, 1985.

Alam, Khurshed: The Economoic Development of Assam Since Independence—An Analytical Study, Gauhati University, 1975.

Bagchi, Jayanta Kumar: Regional Co-operative Among Jute Production Counties, Gauhati University, 1984.

Baishya, Prabin: The Role of Small Scale and Cottage Industries—A Case Study in Kamrup Districts, Gauhati University, 1986.

Barman, Kandarpa Kumar: A Critical Study of Agricultural Productivity in Assam (1951–78), Gauhati University, 1986.

Barthakur, Shrikanta: Problems of Transportation System in the North Eastern Region of India with Special Reference to the Containerised Movement of Selected Groups of Exportable Commodities, Gauhati University, 1990.

Barua, Runumi: Intersectoral Balances in India's Planned Economic Development with Special Reference to Assam, Gauhati University, 1986.

Barua, Srinath: A critical Analysis of Planned Economic Development of India with Reference to Assam (1951–74)—An Econometric Approach, Gauhati University, 1978.

Barua, Sunil: A Study on Certain Problems of Fertility Among the Khasi Women of Meghalaya, Gauhati University, 1981.

Bhambra, Amarjeet Singh: Management of Working Capital in State Undertakings of Assam—An Enquiry into its Problems, Gauhati University, 1990.

Bhatia, P.: Mechanisation of Agriculture in Cachar, Gauhati University, 1978.

Bhowmick, B.C.: Analysis of Risk in Farm Production in Kamrup District, Assam: A Parametric Risk Programming Approach, IARI, New Delhi, 1983.

Bhattacharyya, Asit Ranjan: Panchayati Raj in Tripura with Special Reference to Panisagar Community Development, Gauhati University, 1981.

Bhattacharyya, Dipak: Growth of Tripura's Economy during the Period 1951–74, Calcutta University, 1981.

Bhattacharyya, Gayatri: Impact of Refugee Rehabilitation on Tripura's Economy, Calcutta University, 1981.

Bhattacharyya, Pranab Kr.: Indo-Soviet Economic Relationship (1965–1978), Gauhati University, 1984.

Bhattacharyya, P.R.: Significance of Income Leakages in the Export Base Model of Tripura, Calcutta University, 1981.

Bhuyan, Mahesh: Immigrant Population in Assam: An Analytic-Synthetic Study with Special Treatment of Darrang District, Gauhati University, 1978.

Bhuyan, Prafull Kumar: State Finances of Assam Government During the Plan Period (1951–1952 to 1965–1966), Dibruhgarh University, 1977.

Bora, Debendra Nath: problems and Prospects of Sugar Industry in Assam Co-operative Sugar Mills Ltd, Barua Damungaon, Gauhati University, 1990.

Borah, Ajit Kumar: Pattern of Land Utilization in Assam, Gauhati University, 1981.

Borah, Chandra Kanta: Input Structure and Agricultural Development in Assam—A Case Study on Regional Variations, Dibruhgarh University, 1989.

Borah, Kumud Ch.: Income Distribution, Saving and Expenditure Patterns in the Rural Economy of Assam, Dibruhgarh University, 1978.

Begum, Syeda Hasna Ara: A Socio-Economic Study in Selected Areas in Greater Guwahati, Gauhati University, 1982.

Bezbarua, Rupak: Economic Aspects of Green Leaf Plucking with Special Reference to Work Study in Tea Plantation in North East India, Dibruhgarh University, 1990.

Bordoloi, Buddindranath: A Study of the Problems of Transfer and Alienation of Tribal Land in Assam with Special Reference to the Karbis of the Karbi Anglong District, Dibruhgarh University, 1989.

Bordoloi, Gopal: Population Composition in Assam (1901–1961), Gauhati University, 1978.

Borthakur, Inderjit Kaur: Problems of Agricultural Development in Arunachal (with Special Reference to Subansiri District), Gauhati University, 1975.

Borthakur, Jitendra Kr.: Demography and Socio-Economic Process in Arunchal Pradesh, Gauhati University, 1978.

Chakraborty, Sonali: Urban Fertility in Assam: A Case Study of Dibruhgarh Town, Dibruhgarh University, 1989.

Chakraborty, Sisir: The Demographic Aspects of the Economic Development of Cachar (1951–74), Gauhati University, 1982.

Das, Dipak Kumar: Sales Tax in Meghalaya: An Analytical Study, Gauhati University, 1987.

Das, Manmohan: Structural Analysis of Peasant Agriculture in Assam, Gauhati University, 1980.

Das, Rabindranath: The Role of the Assam State Co-operative Marketing and Consumers Federation Ltd. (Statefed) in the Co-operative Movement in Assam Gauhati University, 1990.

Chaliha, Jyoti Prasad: Pattern of Land Holding and Problems of Investments in Agriculture in Assam—A Case Study in Dibruhgarh District, Dibruhgarh University, 1980.

Chatterjee, Sankar: Interdependence of Outputs and Prices between Assam and the Rest of India, Gauhati University, 1987.

Choudhuri, Bibhash Ranjan: Socio-Economic Problems of Cachar Since Parition, Gauhati University, 1982.

Choudhuri, H.: Consumption Pattern of the Households in Assam: An Econometric Study, Gauhati University, 1980.

Choudhuri, Rabindra Kr.: Public Expenditure in Assam During 1951–1966: An Analytical Study Gauhati University, 1976.

Choudhuri, Tushar Kanti: Population Trends in Assam Since 1931—A Regional Study, Gauhati University, 1971.

Datta Choudhuri, Arun Kr.: Some Aspects of Socio-Economic Conditions of Karimganj Since Independence with Special Reference to Community Development, Gauhati University, 1982.

Dutta, Bidhu Bhushan: Economic Development Through Banking—A Case Study of Meghalaya, Gauhati University, 1984.

Dutta, P.C.: Problems and Prospects of Silk Production in Assam with Special Reference to Sibsagar District, Dibruhgarh University, 1989.

Dutta, Siba Kanta: Role of Panchayat Level Co-operative Societies in Rural Development of Assam: A Politico-Economic Study (A Case Study of Dibruhgarh District) Dibruhgarh University, 1989.

Deka, Bandhu Ram: Agricultural Credit in Assam—A Study on Institutional Sources from 1951 to 1974, Gauhati University, 1986.

Deka, Golak Chandra: The Role of Life Insurance (LIC) of India in the North-Eastern Region Gauhati University, 1987.

Dey, Kripa Sondhu: Measurement of Human Fertility in Assam, Gauhati University, 1977.

Dey, N.K.: Contribution of Homestead and Orchards to Family Income in Assam: A Case Study of Tinsukia Sub-Division of Dibruhgarh District, Dibruhgarh University, 1986.

Dey, Ratna: Land Revenue Administration in Cachar During British Rule (1832–1900), Gauhati University, 1989.

Dhar, Pranab Kumar: Financing Assam's Plan, Gauhati University, 1981.

Goel, Niranjan Prasad: Demographic Structure of North-East India, NEHU, 1983.

Gogoi, Girin: Urbanisation in Assam (1901–1971), Dibruhgarh university, 1986.

Goswami, Atul: Prices and Cost of Living in Assam (1951–1970), Gauhati University, 1975.

Goswami, Hirendra: Land Reforms in India Since Independence with Special Reference to Assam, Gauhati University, 1985.

Goswami, Homeswar: Population Trends in the Brahmaputra Valley of Assam (1881–1931), Dibrugarh University, 1976.

Goswami, Nani Gopal: Financial Management of Tea Estates in Assam : A Case Study in Sibsagar and Dibruhgarh District, Dibruhgarh University, 1990.

Goswami, Pranay Jyoti: Socio-Economic Life of Plain Tribal Communities in the Barak Valley, The Extent of Transition, Gauhati University, 1989.

Guha, Thakurta, S.N.: Contract Labour in Construction Industries: An Empirical Study with Reference to Tripura, Calcutta University 1972.

Halder, Gopal: Economic Problems of Tripura with Special Reference to its Population Since, 1974, North Bengal University, 1983.

Huda, Manirul: Sibsagar Town: A Study in Urbanization, Dibruhgarh University, 1979.

Jha, S.D.: Socio-Economic Study of Arunachal Pradesh, Gauhati University, 1976.

Kalita, Jayashree Das: Role of Commercial Bank in the Agricultural Development of Assam Since Nationalization—A Case Study of District of Sonitpur, Gauhati University, 1990.

Kalita, Krishna Kanta: Co-operative as the Booster of Rural Development: The Role of Gaon Panchayat Level Co-operative Societies of the District of Kamrup, Gauhati University, 1987.

Kar, Biman: Economic Development of Tripura From 1951 to 1966—A critical Study, Gauhati University, 1975.

Kar, Ganesh Chandra: Problems of Agricultural Labourers in Assam Since Independence, Gauhati University, 1975.

Kar, Parimal Ch.: Socio-Economic Life of the Garos in Transition, Gauhati University, 1979.

Khan, Sakiya: India's Balance of Payment Since Independence (1947–77), Gauhati University, 1984.

Khatun, Ramiza: Land Reforms in India Since Independence with Special Reference to Assam, Gauhati University, 1985.

Lahiri, Ranjan Kr.: Family Farming in a Developing Economy: A Study Based on Farm Management Survey of Tripura, Kalyani University, 1976.

Lakhar, B.C.: Socio-Economic Profile of a Tribal Community in an Urban Fringe, Dibruhgarh University, 1987.

Mahanta, Pranab Kr.: Problems of Urban Areas of Assam, Gauhati University 1985.

Majumdar, Apurbananda: Electronic Industry in India: Reviews of Strategy and Growth, Gauhati University, 1987.

Md, Islamuddin: Problems and Prospects of Agricultural Marketing in Manipur During Plan Period 1951 to 1952–1984 to 1985, Manipur University, 1985.

Mohonta, Trishna: Foreign Aid and India's Economic Development, Gauhati University, 1976.

Misra, Bani Prasanna: Socio-Economic Adjustment of Tribals: A Case Study of Tripura Jhumias, Gokhale Institute, Poona, 1972.

Misra, Bishnu Prasad: Management Principles and Techniques in India: A Case Study of Tea Industries in Assam, Dibruhgarh University, 1981.

Nair, M.K. Sukumaran: Agrarian Relations and Transition in Meghalaya, NEHU, 1984.

Nath, Binoy Kumar: State Trading in Assam—An Analytical Study, Gauhati University, 1983.

Neog, Ajit Kurmar: Rural Unemployment in Assam with Special Reference to Kamrup District Gauhati University, 1990.

Pai, V. Santosh: Lead Bank Service in Assam with Special Reference to Kamrup District, Gauhati University, 1987.

Passah, Philomath: Some Aspects of the Economy of Meghalaya, Gauhati University, 1982.

Pathak, Bhabendra Nath: Road Transport in the North Eastern Region of India (1951–76), Gauhati University, 1980.

Phukan, Minoti: Socio-Economic Status of the Women Labour in the Tea-Garden of Assam, Assam Agricultural University, 1987.

Phukan, Umananda: Socio-Economic Problems of the Ex-Tea Garden Labour Population in Assam, Gauhati University, 1977.

Poon, Khagendra Kr.: Indo-Nepal Economic Relationship with Special Reference to Indo-Nepal Trade Since 1951, Gauhati University, 1981.

Roy, Dipankar: Configuration of Poverty in the Border Areas of Meghalaya: A Case Study of Shella, NEHU, 1987.

Roy, Khirendra Ch.: The Newspaper Industry in Assam Since 1947—A Critical Study, Gauhati University, 1984.

Roy, Ram Chandra: Small Farmers of Assam: An Enquiry into Their Problems During the Plan Period, Gauhati University, 1985.

Saha, Niranjan: The Economics of Shifting Cultivation in Assam, Gauhati University, 1972.

Sahariah, Bhubaneswar: Interregional Population Interaction in Assam: A Demographic Appraisal, Gauhati University,1988.

Saikia, Anil: A Study of Human Mortality in Assam, Dibruhgarh University, 1989.

Saikia (Bora), Anima: Progress, Problems and Prospects of Multi-Purpose Co-operative Societies Case Study in Assam, Gauhati University, 1989.

Saikia, Anuva: Female Participation in Agricultural Operation in Assam—A Study of Sibsagar District, Gauhati University, 1983.

Saikia, Paban Ch.: Socio-Economic Structure of a Dibongiya Village in Assam, Gauhati University, 1973.

Saikia, Sunil Kr.: Professional Management in State Undertakings of Assam—Its Growth Handicaps and Prospects, Gauhati University, 1989.

Saikia, Trailkya Nath: Surplus Manpower in Agriculture in Assam, Dibruhgarh University, 1975.

Saraf, Giridharilal: The Role of State in India's Industrial Development (1951–76), Gauhati University, 1982.

Sarma, Archana: levels of Living in Assam (1955–1980), Dibruhgarh University, 1989.

Sarma, Bhupen: An Investigation in to the Fuctioning of Assam Small Industries Development Corporation From 1962 to 1982, Gauhati University, 1990.

Sarma, Kailash Ch.: Rural Credit in Assam—A Study of Nalbari Sub-Division, Gauhati University, 1974.

Sarma, Madhab: Commodity Flows in the Tinsukia Division of North-East Frontier Railways: A Study of Spatial Trading Patterns, Dibruhgarh University, 1984.

Sarma, Prabin Kumar: Role of Forest Resources on the Economy of Assam, Dibruhgarh University, 1986.

Sarma, B.: Economic Organisation of Tribal Agriculture with Special Reference to North-East India, Bombay University, 1980.

Seetha, Pendyala: Public Co-Operation in Assam—An Analytical Study Since 1960, Gauhati University, 1980.

Seleh, Swabers Islam: Nagaland's Economics in Transition Since 1964, Gauhati University, 1984.

Sharma, Monoranjan: Public Enterprises in Assam: An Analytical Study of Their Role in the Industrial Development of the State, Dibruhgarh University, 1985.

Sharma, Atul Ch.: A study of Assam Finance: Structure and Trend (1947–1966), Gauhati University, 1972.

Sharma, Arun: Impact of Community Development Block on Rural Development: A Comparative Study of Chakai (Bihar) and Dimoria (Assam) Blocks, Gauhati University, 1990.

Singh, Chongthan Budhi: Fishing Economic of the Thanga: A Lake Dwelling Peasant Community of Manipur, Gauhati University, 1973.

Singh, H. Nabakishor: The Industrial Policy of the Government of India Since Independence, Gauhati University, 1970.

Singh, Hawaibam Biren: A Comparative Study of Socio-Economic Transition of Tribal and NonTribal People of Manipur During Post—Independence Period, Gauhati University, 1989.

Singha, Jagadish Ch.: Socio-Economic Development of the United Khasi and Jaintia Hills and Garo Hills Since Independence, Gauhati University, 1979.

Singh, L. Brajamandol: Population Growth and Occupational Pattern in a Development Process of the Economy of the Scheduled Tribes in Manipur (1951–!981), Manipur University, 1987.

Singh, L. Krishnamangol: Economic Change in Manipur: Leading Issues in Development, Manipur University, 1987.

Singh, M. Iboton: The Economic Development Manipur (Since 1939), Gauhati University, 1970.

Singh, N. Ram: Agricultural Development in the North Eastern Region of India Including Sikkim During the Plan Period, Manipur University, 1988.

Singh, Thounaojam Surjabaran: Budgetary Trends in Manipur (1951–1966), Gauhati University, 1975.

Singh, W. Kumar: Population Growth and Agricultural Development in Manipur (1951–1985), Manipur University, 1985.

Thangliana, R.: Occupational Mobility Among the Mizos, NEHU, 1986.

Todi, Bhagawati Prasad: Sales Taxation in North East India, Gauhati University, 1990.

Vincent, Kaushal: Socio-Economic Study of a Growth Centre Bhoilymbong—A Village in Meghalaya, Gauhati University, 1976.

EPILOGUE

Economics is a behavioural science. Therefore, research in Economics is intended to firstly, display the reality of changing human behaviour into theoretical frame and secondly, to apply the abstraction of reality in order to explain the economic behaviour of economic agents under varying situations. The foregoing review of research in Economics presents the work done during the period 1970–90, in north eastern region of India. The purpose of this survey was to give a brief account of major issues in the fields of research in economics. For this purpose, more than two hundred research works were reviewed and more than hundred Ph.D. research titles were scanned and analysed. It is assumed that more than three hundred titles form a significantly large sample size and could be considered as a representative sample of available research work in the region in the field of Economics. On the basis of this assumption, this work would reflect a bird's eye view of the major trends and status of research in Economics in the north eastern part of India. In order to reveal the extent of specialised treatment within the purview of the discipline, the research works have been classified into ten major, well known recognised branches of Economics.

The largest proportion of research output is available in the field of Economic Development, Agricultural Economics and Economic Planning. Lesser number representing the fields of Public Finance, Production Technology, Trade and Transport Economics. This distribution is not surprising as north-east economy is still characterised mainly as agricultural and rural based economy with less degree of development of modernise sector. But it is surprising that this region has vast mineral, forest and other natural resources, but the studies relating to resource economics are available only a few in number.

In the era of economic reforms and liberalisation at national level, the economies of north-east would also begin to modernise their economic sectors, through industrialisation, so new research fields would hopefully emerge and would get proper attention of the economists. For instance, research efforts in the fields of infra-structural economics, inter-industrial economics, trade and service sector economics would be helpful in appreciating the regional economic issues and aspirations, problems and perspectives in coming future.

Increasing rate of growth of research works done in the region along with time during the study period reveals that the awareness towards higher education and research is spreading speedily in all the north-eastern states. Therefore, the facilities and opportunities are also emerging in the region to meet the supply and demand of skilled and educated manpower. Statewise distribution of research output demonstrates that among the seven states, largest number of studies are available for the state Assam, followed by Meghalaya. Least number of reviewed literature available from Arunachal Pradesh and Mizoram. It is worthwhile to mention that availability of research works has a strong association with the number of active research institutions and university departments in the state.

Three major sources of published research works are books, articles published in edited volumes and articles published in various research journals. Out of the total research titles reviewed, books and articles published in edited volumes, constitute the largest component, rest are the articles published in various research journals. Research articles are mostly published in Economic and Political Weekly, Manpower, Social Action, Indian Journal of Agricultural Economics and other well reputed journals of national standard. These journals are widely circulated in India and abroad. If more research output is getting chance to publish in these and other journals, then more and more social scientists from rest of India would be aware of major economic issues and problems of north-eastern part of India. This would lead to attract the due attention among the academicians at large.

Research is a continuous process, whereby using of scientific techniques, disaggregated data and appropriate research methodology, there is always a scope of improvement. It is hoped that economists of the region would continue to strengthen their efforts to expose themselves, to study and address the complex economic realities of the region.